TRUTH ON THE RUN

KATE SANTORO

Truth on the Run

First Edition

Published by Kate Santoro

Printed in the United States of America

Hardcover ISBN: 9798-9996063-1-0

Softcover (Paperback) ISBN: 979-8-9996063-0-3

Cover designed by Peter Kennedy

Edited by Melissa Colasanti

This is a work of nonfiction. The experiences and lessons shared are based on the author's personal journey. Any references to individuals or events are either factual or used in a transformative way.

DEDICATION

Ger, this book is dedicated to you, my man. A gifted soul, reader, writer, and a unique thinker. A man whose words had so much weight, a life cut too short to use them. You are physically gone now, but your voice, smile, and words echo in my bones. Your way with the English language —it will never leave. Thank you for being my teacher. You told me to write, to tell a story, to be myself, so here it is. It's not easy to do, but this one's for you, brother. Not because it's polished—because it's real.

I can see your smile now, dimples on your cheeks, looking a little smug and arrogant, like a brilliant guy would. Maybe—just maybe— you will teach us all to remember how to write, and how to think, process, and feel with pen and paper. I wish I could see you now, Ger. I wish I could hear you say, "Kate, let's go do that." But I know, in my heart, there is no end to your story, Gerry. No end to the love we feel for you.

You are flying free now, free as a bird. I can't catch up yet, but I will see you again.

You made my life far more meaningful, more curious, more fun, more interesting.

You made me me. Showed me to challenge the status quo, to never do it half way.

We Epcotted Epcot together, we played hoops, we did mischief, we went to parties together, and you, as a devoted loving father and teacher, were a role model to your children. Every summer when you'd visit, you'd say, "Kate, good God, totally, write that down."

"Write that down."

Three hundred and fifty hours ago, when I heard your voice in the middle of the night, I grabbed seven notebooks, went to the library, and I've been writing ten hours a day ever since.

Your voice will forever stick.

Ger, I miss your spirit. Wish I could have said a real goodbye. Rest in eternal peace, my sweet brother. I love you.

CONTENTS

Acknowledgments   vii
Author's Note   ix
Preface   xiii

1. CHOICES   1
    Move-In Day, Welcome to L.A., Willie's Two-Hundred-
    Dollar Haircut, and a Brown-Haired Identity Crisis   4

2. LONDON: TWO HEARTS, ONE HOPE   7
    July 2008, Chelsea Westminster Hospital   11
    August 7, 2008   13
    Shock   14

3. THE DARK CAVE   23
4. DIGGING OUT   29

5. QUESTIONS ASKED, MIRACLES ANSWERED   33
    So Keep Going   39

6. BACK TO BEANTOWN: A REBIRTH   43
    August 25, 2009   44

7. LACING UP AND LEANING IN   51
8. FOOTFALLS AND FRIENDSHIP   55
9. THE BOSTON MARATHON BOMBING, 2013:
    WHEN THE WORLD STOPS RUNNING   61

10. FROM SIX-MINUTE MILES TO MOTION ON
    PAUSE   65
    Park City, Utah   65
    ACL/MCL SURGERY   67

11. BOSTON IN MY BONES   71
    April 15, 2019   71

12. THE BEAUTIFUL RIPPLE EFFECTS OF GRIEF   75
    The Power of True Kindness   76
    Find Your Magic   77

13. FACE YOUR FEARS EVEN WHEN YOU'RE
    CLUELESS AND SCARED SHITLESS   79
14. UPROOTED: A NEW START LINE   83

15. LET'S TALK ABOUT PUSHING THROUGH YOUR
    MILE TWENTY-THREE   89
    Mile Twenty-Three: When Body & Mind Break   90
    Where the Real Work Begins   93
    Here's What Mile Twenty-Three Taught Me   94
    Stop Living Small   100
    Finish What You Start   102

16. SETBACKS, SUNSHINE, AND STARTING OVER   105

17. THE PALISADES WILDFIRES—CHAOS AND
    COMMUNITY UNITED   113
    The Day the Fire Came   113
    11:11 on the PCH, Make a Wish   115
    11:40 a.m.   117
    The Same Tears   119
    Ancient Stairs   122
    Manhattan Beach   124

18. A LETTER TO MY PARENTS   127
    My Dad: "The Quiet Champion"   131

19. THE WILD ONES   135

20. THE ART OF TIMING   139
    February 2020   141

21. DIGGING IN TO DIG OUT   145
22. MY RIGHT-HAND MAN: THE ART OF
    LOVING LONG   149
23. PARENTING AND PEOPLE SHOWING UP:
    COMPASSION   153
24. MEMORIES ARE YOUR HOME   161
25. GOLF, SHALL WE?   165

26. THE BRIGHT SIDE OF KIND STRANGERS IN
    THE DARK   175
    August 8, 2023   178

ACKNOWLEDGMENTS

To Paul, my Italian Stallion; my five loving children; Gerry's four children; Melissa, my editor; Lucy and Riley's godmamas; my run partner and run buddies; special Beantown buddies; and the kind people and amazing strangers I meet along the way. It's never by accident who shows up in your life.

To my mother—slipping away from this world on the very same day my twin sons were born into it.

Life gives. Life takes. Sometimes, in the exact same breath. You can't plan it. You can't reason with it. But you can pay attention. Because those moments—the wild, strange ones that make no sense—are never random. They're the secret stitches in the fabric of your life. The threads you can't see but always feel.

AUTHOR'S NOTE

Whatever brings you here, welcome. This is not a book of how-tos or neatly packaged inspiration. This is a book of truth on the run—written in motion, written from the mess. This is a book about the kind of faith that shows up when there is absolutely no map. When the diagnosis is terrifying, the money runs out, or your town literally burns down. When you have to trust without proof, without control, without clarity. That's the muscle I've had to build. And I'll tell you—it wasn't built in a yoga class or a weekend retreat. It was built in emergency rooms, at kitchen tables, through late-night cries, and early morning runs, where the only thing I could do was move my legs and pray.

If you're reading this right now, maybe you're sitting in a similar place: unsure, tired, overwhelmed, grieving, starting over. Or maybe you're just curious. So I'm starting here with blind faith because before I could rebuild, before I could find joy, before I could write anything, I had to trust in something I couldn't see—and maybe, just maybe, so do you.

The real story is what those miles gave me—perspective. The kind of clarity that only shows up when you're breathless, undone, and stripped down enough to see what actually matters.

But the miles aren't the headline.

I'm not a Princeton writer; I'm not a famous author. There's no hashtag after my name, but what I do have is a well-earned perspective—one that's been tested, pushed, flipped upside down, and still somehow found its way forward.

I'm a proud mom of five amazing children, a wife, and a woman with more real-life experiences than I ever asked for—enough to fill seven notebooks, phone notes, conversations, breakdowns, and belly laughs.

People told me for years, "You should write a book." Yet between moving cross-country, handling medical emergencies, showing up for my family, and making sure nobody ran out of clean socks or emotional support, I didn't exactly have a clear calendar. So I jotted things down here and there—scraps of thoughts on napkins, notebooks, the backs of receipts—and eventually, I gathered them all together, and this book was born.

Now, maybe you're also the type who thinks you've got it all figured out. So was I.

I used to believe in planning everything, controlling what I could, and getting out ahead of disaster. But life doesn't care how smart you are or what you think you know. It'll throw a curveball when you're not looking—and sometimes even when you are. It'll humble you, stretch you, and gift you moments of grace amid the mess.

So yeah, if you've got a big title, a perfect résumé, or an alphabet soup of degrees—this book is still for you. Especially for you, because no matter where you come from, we all have something to learn from one another. And no matter how much we think we know, there's always more truth to uncover—especially when you're running.

So here it is—my truth on the run. I can finally say it out loud: I have never had the luxury of time. Not real time. Not the kind of time that sits with you. The kind that doesn't ask for anything back. The kind that isn't interrupted by barking dogs, groceries, or people needing something.

For thirty years now, my time, mind, heart, and soul have belonged to someone or something else. That's not a complaint—it's just the truth. One I carried with grace. One I have been proud to carry. But it meant that this, right now—sitting in a library, writing with a pen in one notebook and then another and then another—this is heaven.

This is the rarest of rare, uninterrupted days. There is nobody else's cadence of thought to work around. No talking. Just me and my thoughts and the rhythm of the pen.

No timer. No pickup line. No deadline.

Just my words pouring out like they've been waiting three decades to be invited in.

Maybe you're not a runner—never laced up sneakers, pinned a bib to your shirt, or crossed a finish line with tears in your eyes and blood in your shoes. Yet I bet you've run. Run from fear. Run toward hope, dreams. Run with love on your back and pain in your chest.

We all run. And we all crash. But the miracle is not in avoiding the fall—it's in the rising. The rebuilding. The return. This book began in grief, but it ends in fire. Not the kind that destroys, but the kind that fuses. That forges gold out of iron. That lights the path forward.

You are not alone.

You are not broken. You are simply at mile twenty-three—sore, scared, blistered, but still standing.

So keep going.

Run with your bloody shoes, your bruised soul, your heart wide open.

That's where life really begins. That's the go.

At some point, many parts of our lives become more about grieving than growing.

You don't plan for it, but you feel it. The layers slowly stack. Loss after loss.

Then your town goes up in flames and takes your home, structure, and life belongings with it—and all the things you thought you'd carry forever are gone.

It comes in waves, but it doesn't leave. It just makes space for the next one.

Over time, I just stopped fighting it.

I have learned to use grief as a portal to move forward.

It's how I show up for others as they begin their reckoning.

This book—this whole damn effort—is my offering to the ones still carrying the weight.

It's a dedication to the Palladian community.

To friends and my brother's family, who will be grieving for the rest of their lives.

Not just for what is gone—but for what won't return.

Grief doesn't get easier, but I've learned to meet it with a loving heart, open hands, and peace.

To let it change me in a better way, instead of breaking me.

And to keep going—not despite it, but because of it.

PREFACE

Over the last twenty-plus years, I've run approximately 23,083 miles. That's not a humblebrag; it is just the plain truth. That's roughly one full lap around the Earth, training for and racing about thirty marathons and a couple dozen shorter races—from 5Ks, 10Ks, 15Ks, half-marathons, triathlons, Swim Across Americas, dirt trails, pavement, beaches, bogs, bridges, and trails—with every surface and distance in between. Being knocked down so many times I gave up counting.

I have found myself surrounded by a pattern of death, tragedies, faith, mysteries and miracles, bicoastal moves, wildfires, bad accidents you can't make up, and bombs at marathon finish lines.

The story doesn't just represent the miles—it represents decades of discipline, transformation, and truth discovered one footstep at a time.

Our town was recently wiped out by a wildfire, and there have been home displacements since January. But me? I am doing just fine—enlightened and ready to share.

Why? Because this is the story of life again and again.

I had to share my stories for fun's sake alone, but the real story is what I have gained on the road. The tribulations and miles gave me perspective.

A damn good, strong, confident perspective—one I have to share.

The one with a kind of clarity that shows up when you're breathless, undone, and stripped down enough to see what actually matters.

> "Do not let your fire go out, spark by irreplaceable spark, in the hopeless swamps of the approximate, the not quite, the not yet, the not at all. Do not let the hero in your soul perish, in lonely frustration for the life you deserved, but have never been able to reach. Check your road and the nature of your battle." —Ayn Rand

1

CHOICES

How do we ever know if we've made the right choices? Especially the risky ones. The ones no polite person would recommend at dinner. The ones when you can't even see the edge of the outcome because the fog of "what if" hangs too thick?

Sometimes, we can make a decision like runners in the dark. No finish line lit up. No promise of water stations. Just the sound of our breath and the thud of our footfalls on uncertain ground.

Maybe you moved across the country. Maybe you married the person everyone quietly doubted. Maybe you signed up for a marathon with a soft tissue injury, a shoe that didn't fit, or a heart that wasn't ready.

Maybe you said yes when it would have been safer—easier—to say no. And now you wonder: Did I pick the right race? The right road? Will this end in joy or just another blister?

But here's the quiet truth you learn when you run long enough: You don't get to know at the start. You only ever know in the middle. In the sweat and the struggle. In the mile eighteen doubts and the mile twenty-four grace.

Risky choices are like marathons. You commit early. You pay later.

And the bill comes in strange currency—lessons, losses, unexpected joys. None of it is guaranteed. All of it is yours.

So how do we know if we made the right call? Maybe the only real way is to keep going and find out.

Oh, this is rich.

This is so true on the run. The sooner we surrender to asking the real question—*what am I actually in control of?*—the sooner we make peace with it, the sooner we'll understand the hardest truth of all: We're not steering the big picture.

And that's brutal to learn. It was brutal for me. Because when you've painted a perfect picture in your mind and life hands you the opposite . . . well, that's not a failure. That's education. A long, humbling, soul-stretching lesson you never signed up for, but it shapes you all the same.

After fifty-four years on life's roller coaster, after some bad timing, some traumatic circumstances, a well-placed slap from the universe, and miles upon miles to think it all through, I've come to realize: life doesn't show up the way you pictured.

It arrives wild, sideways, and unscheduled, and whether you're ready for it or not, it teaches.

My husband was an only child, content and satisfied. As a happily married couple, we never talked about the size of family we wanted. And after two healthy children by the age of twenty-nine, a strong career path, and a girl and a boy, he said, "Great, perfect, right Kate? We are good."

I never answered that question because the more I became a mother, the deeper I let myself sink into it, and the more I wanted it. All of it.

I'd sit on the floor with my kids, balls and puzzles scattered across the floor. As I watched little hands stack, learn, run, and tumble, their little faces lit up every day with new discoveries. Playgrounds and museums in Boston were my happiest of days.

That's when I saw it: this was the joy. This was the thing I hadn't seen coming.

It wasn't the job title, money, the meetings, or the carefully crafted résumé I wanted. It was this. More of this. I didn't want to race away from it. I wanted more kids. More life. More mess. More small hands grabbing mine.

I thought I was building a side career. But I was building a family.

Our youngest boy, Will, was the game changer; his smile and spark brought joy twenty-four hours a day. Will's magic guided me forward to see that the best gift I could give him in life was a sibling. Willie had too much to offer to be the bookend to our family chapter.

I could not adapt for a while here.

Culturally, L.A. was not at all what I thought it would be; it was like joining a SoulCycle class with no friends. Everyone knew the moves. I was just trying to clip in without losing a limb and find my way around. A brand-new zip code I could not remember mid-ride. It didn't take more than five minutes to notice the difference.

In Boston, when someone says, "I'll be there at 7," they mean 6:50 —with their coat on, ready to help you carry chairs or shovel your driveway. You make a plan; you show up. No drama. No maybes. California runs on an entirely different clock. Plans? A suggestion.

I was vulnerable, brand-new, and fresh out of friends, overwhelmed with wanting to make it all feel right. I tried.

Here it's, "Let's totally get together!" and "We should grab coffee sometime!" "Take a hike?" with big, blinding smiles . . . and then nothing. Total silence. Like tossing a text into the ocean and waiting for it to float back.

Plans? They are more of an idea out here. A soft breeze. A "we'll see how the universe feels tomorrow" kind of thing. A suggestion with no confirmation.

I wasn't at all used to this airiness, this beautiful, polite flakiness.

Back home, you made plans like you made pasta, firm, hot, ready by six. Here, plans were more like kale water—vague, green, and probably not real, mostly forgotten about.

Then I'd torture myself with a comparison game.

Back east, I had rhythm, certainty, history, sturdy roots in the ground, a tribe, and extended family. People who understood me. If I showed up late in ripped sweats with mascara down my face, it did not matter. I was just "having a week."

Real friends in midlife? It's like dating without the wine and a lot more judgment. Everyone's already booked. Busy. They have had their "mom squads" for decades, Pilates cliques, book clubs, and wine nights you are not invited to, and if you are, it feels like you're not supposed to be there. I'm supposed to be . . . what? Evolving? Like an accidental tourist in my own life.

I could barely remember the passwords to my computer or find my keys and clicker to the driveway gate. Who would want to be this woman's friend?

Certainly not me. I get it.

I don't do fluff. My hair gets done at KC Beauty Academy in Koreatown, not Beverly Hills. Or I do it myself, hunched over the bathroom sink like a scene from a low-budget action film. And honestly? I love it because in this city of filters, there's a true quality layer most people miss. They are here but just a lot harder to find.

Move-In Day, Welcome to L.A., Willie's Two-Hundred-Dollar Haircut, and a Brown-Haired Identity Crisis

When we first landed at LAX at the end of COVID, there was a rental car strike. We sat on the airport curb for two and a half hours with two dogs, fifteen bags, three sets of golf clubs, and a dog having a seizure. Riley was crying, saying, "I want to go home." My husband, who's always smooth, looked totally unglued.

Instead of rising up and helping, I folded. Got a little bitchy.

The ugly, mean mom came out alive and kicking, and to say it was not a smooth entry would be an understatement. So here we are. After a six-hour flight and three hours of waiting, we pull up to this old Spanish rental home. Our lifelong and only belongings sardined into a storage container.

Lesson 1. Do not go into a plan you agreed to with a cynical, critical mind.

The rental had squeaky old beds.

Bad vibes. You could feel it—the house had been through a divorce. He was a cinematographer for *Black Hawk Down*—and this lady must've been angry. It was dark. But it fit the bill. And we only had it for three months. I thought it would be no problem to buy a house in

L.A. in three months. Easy, right? Well, the market increased thirty percent that year. Every single time we'd go to look at a house, it was already gone. And I had the nerve to tell one realtor: "Oh sorry, I don't play that game. I'm from Boston." Yeah. Shut up, lady. The house was gone.

Everybody here is a cash buyer. And nobody really gave a shit about us.

Like an idiot, I thought, they just have to get to know us, maybe? Thought going on Nextdoor would help. So there I went—and got totally swindled by realtors and side hustles. Everyone with an angle, everyone wanting something.

So, OK, maybe I get braver.

I printed a note, a photo, and put notes under forty people's doors. That didn't work either. Before we knew it, our plan A went to plan B and we had to go to another rental for six months—just to square away a place to buy.

Will was an absolute champ, the opposite of me, celebrating every new swag friend, place, and change in his life. He got immediate invites to parties and started surfing. He even got handpicked for commercials. With no driving permit, he knew the beat and melted into it while I was frozen thirty steps behind him. I thought, who is teaching who how to behave now?

He was entering into a new school as a junior in high school and wanted a haircut.

Simple enough, right? Just a trim, nothing fancy. So I asked a neighbor, and this young, gorgeous girl came to the house—yes, a house call haircut, which should've been the first red flag. She was like a movie star, boobies right in Will's face. Will loved it, and then she handed me the bill. Two hundred dollars for a boy's trim? Just a clip clip, thanks, ma'am. Welcome to the West Coast.

But it gets better . . .

The second and only time, I needed a small something, just a refresh, just some soft highlights to help me feel human again. The matted dreadlock was back, now gray. I asked another neighbor who told me to hire another woman. The woman turned my entire head of hair a dark chocolate brown—not soft, not subtle. Just dark brunette.

Full send. I looked in the mirror and blinked twice. Like who is that? Does she have a hearing problem on highlights?

Then I showed up to my first Loyola Mothers' Guild event at the Bel-Air Bay Club that night, fully brown-haired, freshly relocated, trying to make small talk while holding in a self-conscious laugh.

I laughed at the pathetic me with dark hair and a new zip code and the absurdity of trying to feel at home in a place. They kept surprising me at every turn.

I didn't sit down and plan it out on a whiteboard with bullet points and a vision board because life doesn't ask for permission. It just moves in its own direction, fast and furious. No, I was not in the now, and if you don't move with it in L.A., you get left behind.

2

LONDON: TWO HEARTS, ONE HOPE

We lived in London at the time. My husband, Paul, had a work commitment that brought us overseas for three to five years, or so we thought. After two years of trying, we got pregnant. One sac. One placenta. Two lives in one sac. One terrifying diagnosis. London was as gray and wet as a shine on cement. Cold crept in as I sat in the corner of the room.

Our doctor sat across from us, tipping her glasses with her crisp, white, proper coat. Her face was tight, not the way you want your doctor to look. She cleared her throat. "Kate, you're pregnant." I felt a strange little lift in my chest, then she kept going.

"But this is . . . this is not good news." The air in the room thickened. Heavy. She showed us a cold, clinical chart. Then the words came out a bit seriously and coldly. Like she'd said this too many times before, and it never got easier. "Kate and Paul, this is a dangerous pregnancy. Life-threatening, to be blunt. You have a fifty-fifty chance here—there's roughly a thirty-three percent chance they both survive. Thirty-three percent chance they're born but with serious disabilities. And . . ." She hesitated. I watched her emotional discord, and she continued, "Thirty-three percent chance they both die." Silence. I heard the faint hum of the building. Someone coughed two doors down. The distant London rain wheezed against the window. My heart dropped. Like a stone in a bottomless well.

That was the moment everything changed. Right there. In that gray room, on that gray day, under that gray sky, where hope cracked just enough to let terror in.

The doctor recommended cord occlusion—to save one baby and terminate the other. Medically, yes, cord occlusion made total sense but not emotionally or spiritually. We couldn't do it. We wouldn't do it. We couldn't play God with our two sons who took a year to feel.

To make the judgment call and wonder for the remainder of our lives who we chose to terminate? Even if it was the medically logical thing, even if one twin was struggling, even if carrying both meant we might lose them both, we took our chances.

After that day—the day the words twin-to-twin transfusion syndrome fell like a hammer—we didn't walk out of the hospital the same. Worry settled into our bones. Like the London damp in winter. Cold. Constant. Hard to shake.

I started in the private health care system; then they moved me to Chelsea Westminster Hospital, where I was scanned twice a week for roughly thirty weeks. Morning appointments, hospital stays, surgery two times inside the womb, all within a foreign country, were like following a maze. Sometimes, you make choices in life, then you have to face what is in front of you and deal with it, even when the sun barely bothers to rise. I'd sit on that cold table week after week while the tech rolled the wand across my belly, quietly watching the screen, measuring this, checking that, amniotic fluid amounts, limb length, tiny lungs flickering like fireflies, heartbeats struggling to stay in time.

Nobody ever said much. Just numbers scribbled, a lot of squinting. A nod here. A pause there. I'd hold my breath when they did. At home, the monitor sat beside the bed like some kind of fragile lifeline. I'd press the Doppler against my skin, twisting it slowly, praying for the gallop of two tiny hearts. Some days, I found them quick, racing away like they knew the game was the same with the kicks in the belly. I grew fast and felt healthy, strong, and proud. Twenty weeks came. Then twenty-five. And the doctors didn't say twin-to-twin again. No alarm in their voices. No sharp looks. No clipped warnings.

"Everything looks good," they'd say. "The boys are growing, no issues." And for the first time in a long time, we believed them. In the middle of all that fear, we let the kids get excited. We celebrated milestones. All together, we felt the strong kicks inside my belly after dinner. We hung onto hope, and we were passing hopeful milestones.

We picked out names; we were getting excited despite any negative information. At twenty-five weeks, the docs suggested a laser ablation surgery to prevent any upcoming twin-to-twin transfusion syndrome, which would happen later in the pregnancy.

The surgeon, who specialized in this exact surgery, happened to be in London that week. They felt it was our best-case scenario to carry the boys to term without TTTS. The surgeon was famous for his success saving lives performing this surgery. His name was Professor Kypros Nicolaides, and he was the world's leading fetal medicine specialist and expert in fetoscopic laser surgery for TTTS. He'd been elected to the US National Academy of Medicine for his groundbreaking contributions.

It was a dark, rainy, cold night, and we drove to King's College Hospital. I recall feeling freezing there. My belly was huge, round, and tight with two little lives fighting for space, fighting for time. The older three stayed back with a babysitter. We shielded them from any upsetting information, and off we went.

This was it. That moment, this surgery. That famous doctor. Professor Nicolaides, the best in the world, they said. It was like he was supposed to be the god, but it didn't make us feel any better.

We pulled up. Walked down the long, white hallway that smelled like bleach and fear. They quickly greeted us, no waiting, and led us directly into the operating room. Bright lights. Cold air. Machines blinking and humming like nervous little beats of music. Thirty fellows, doctors in training, were packed like sardines behind the glass wall above me, staring down into that operating room. Like a theater show. Like I was a puppet in the show.

I climbed onto a step, then the table slowly, my body so heavy it felt like dragging a house. Professor Nicolaides came close to my side; he was lovely, kind, calm, confident, steady.

He took my hand. "Katey," he said softly, "I'm going to hold this hand here." His warm fingers wrapped around mine. "And with the other hand . . ."—he smiled gently—"I'm going to go inside of your womb. I want you to be fully aware. Now, look up . . ."

"You'll see their heartbeats here the whole time. Now, Katey, either one of these heartbeats could stop at any point during this surgery. I need you to know that." His voice was low, honest, no sugar. "But if they make it through this, you have a very high chance of bringing home two healthy boys."

As the doctor slipped the laser into my womb, I reached out without thinking—and kissed his hand. It was instinct, like blessing a soldier before battle. Like asking someone to save your life without speaking the words out loud. Then the room filled with sounds. A zap. A zing, pop like a soft crackle, like wires sparking. The smell of burning something deep and human.

Blood, tissue, and heat.

I lay still, staring at the screen, the wand moving inside me, watching the surgery happen in real time like I wasn't the one being opened and lit and mended from the inside out.

On that big screen, in the dim quiet of that surgical room, I saw life and death unfolding in flickering gray shapes. My babies. My body. I swallowed. My throat was dry as paper. I wanted to say something, but words wouldn't come, so I just lay there, staring at the screen. Watching those tiny pulsing hearts. Paul was brave right by my side.

Both of us praying, surrendering. Hoping for a miracle. Numb. Because in that room, under those lights, with thirty pairs of eyes watching and the best doctor in the world holding my hand, there was nothing left to do but believe.

The surgery to cut the blood connection between them was a success. Professor Nicolaides proudly, lovingly, said, "Katey, go now, put your feet up, drink some red wine daily, and expect them on your due date. You're going to be okay. I will send you home with antibiotics in case of infection, yet you should be fine. Expect your two little boys by thirty-two weeks."

Twin-to-twin transfusion syndrome, or TTTS, is one of those medical terms that sounds like it belongs in a textbook until it shows up in your life. It happens only with identical twins who share a placenta. Only the placenta doesn't always know how to divide evenly. One twin gets too much blood—too much fluid, too much pressure on the heart —and the other doesn't get enough. One baby floods; the other starves. It's not just unfair. It's deadly. The donor twin, the one sending blood over, can become severely anemic. That baby's growth slows down, the fluid around them shrinks, and organs can start to shut down. The recipient twin? They're getting overloaded. Their heart is working overtime, and they can go into heart failure just trying to keep up.

This happens inside the womb, quietly and invisibly, all while you're decorating a nursery, raising kids, picking out names, caring for three other children, building a story to end your family chapter, and looking full term by twenty-eight weeks. It's rare, but when it hits, it hits like lightning. And after that kind of experience and education, you never want to hear the word "twin" or think of it the same way again. We ended up needing both laser surgeries.

July 2008, Chelsea Westminster Hospital

I lay alone in this narrow hospital bed, belly stretched tight, heart stretched tighter, far closer to my due date now. It was July.

Paul and the kids had flown back to America. Life, school, and work were still spinning without me. A little loneliness had crept in like water seeping under a door. The walls started pressing closer. No family here. No familiar voices. Just the low buzz of fluorescent lights and the steady beep of monitors.

I couldn't lie there any longer, so I wrapped a thin hospital gown around myself, shuffled into a wheelchair, wheeled myself past the nurses' station, and toward the tiny hospital bookstore tucked near the lobby. The shelves smelled a little bit of paper. My eyes skimmed the titles, not even knowing what I was looking for—until I saw it. A little, soft, beautiful, blue book. *The Power of Now.*

I loved it without knowing why. I bought it along with a Bible and a bright yellow highlighter pen. My hands shook as I paid. After I wheeled myself back to my bed, I opened the pages. I wasn't hunting for answers. God, I was too tired for answers. My brain was tired from too many facts, too many numbers, too many worst-case scenarios. Walls closing in with no familiar voices to break it up.

I needed something else. A tool. A lifeline. The book didn't fix the fear. No, but it gave me something solid to stand on inside the fear.

It became my little anchor in all this confusion and uncertainty. A small, quiet place I could hold onto when everything else felt like sand slipping away.

Somehow, right there, in that hospital bed, in that borrowed gown, with my body breaking and weak and my heart breaking wider, I found a slice of presence. That is a moment I will never forget.

Page after page kept saying, come back to this breath, this heartbeat, this moment, not what might happen, not what already has—just now. Love what is.

It didn't fix the fear, but in that shitty, empty, awful moment, it gave me something to stand on inside of it. A place to sit in the fire without getting fully consumed. A place to breathe when I felt like I was drowning in uncertainty.

That book, that little blue book, became my true anchor. Even in the hospital, even between the prayers, I found a little piece of presence. And in the middle of everything falling apart, that presence was everything. I lay alone in that hospital bed for a week. Two little lives inside me. Just the three of us and the steady beep of the monitors. The days stretched long and slow, like the light outside the window that never seemed to change. Nurses came and went. Meals on plastic trays. Doctors with polite smiles and careful words that circled the truth without landing on it. They never said anything was wrong. Not exactly, but they tiptoed around the edges of it, hunting without speaking. Like maybe the truth was something too sharp to lay flat on the table.

I knew what they weren't saying. This could end in a miracle. Or a tragedy. And in that space—the gap between hope and heartbreak—I found my strange, quiet faith. I kept going back to it. Over and over. Like holding a stone in my hand. This was the only choice I could make: to stay, to wait, to do everything possible to save the lives growing inside of me. Because life is life. Even when the doctors couldn't promise anything. Even when they wouldn't say it out loud. And somehow, with that awful image burned into my mind—the worst-case, the empty arms —I didn't panic. I didn't break. I lay there wrecked and raw but weirdly whole. Holding both truths in my chest at the same time. This could go beautifully right. This could go horribly wrong. And still, I'd be here. Still standing.

Maybe not the same. Maybe cracked wide open but standing. I was hopeful—because the doctors told me to be. Because faith, even fragile, is still faith. And in that strange quiet, I breathed.

Faith was very important to both of us. I'd ask myself, have I done the right thing? Can I live with myself as a woman who chose to not abort a son to save another, to wind up losing both? The answer was simple: I don't know. The lines just aren't clear. Love isn't clean or simple or fair. That's the mystery.

When the doctors tiptoed around the possibility, trying to say what they couldn't quite bring themselves to say, we thought that if we just held on long enough, prayed hard enough, stayed still enough, believed big enough, it would all be okay.

But life doesn't always reward faith with happy endings.

The Power of Now taught me to zoom out just enough to watch the fear without drowning in it. To say: "This is fear. It is hard to feel this pain, but this isn't all of me." It gave me a little breathing room inside the pressure chamber of my life. I wasn't naïve. I knew there were no guarantees, but there was something strangely holy about that calm. Like I was being held by something bigger than I understood.

I still believed we'd all be okay. The due date they were aiming for was the middle to end of August, a planned thirty-two-week scheduled C-section. It was set for around August 18, our oldest son turning nine on August 13.

August 7, 2008

A month later, back home at 3 Pelham Crescent in South Kensington, there was a sudden knock at our door. It was Father Stuart, our priest from St. Mary's. It was a nice surprise. He said he had just returned from Medjugorje. In his beautiful English accent, he said, "Hello, Katey. Is Paul here?"

"No, Father," I said. "He is still at work. What is it, Father?" I asked, a little surprised to see him.

He glanced at me with gentle, uneasy eyes. "Katey, sit down. Please."

I hesitated, feeling a strange seriousness in the air, but I nodded and sat. He stepped closer, resting his hands lightly on my shoulders, his gaze steady and full of care.

"I don't fully understand this," he began softly, "but while I was in Medjugorje, I felt an overwhelming, powerful urge to pray for you and your family. So strong, I couldn't shake it. I knew I needed to come here, to be with you, to pray. Right now. I don't know why—but something in my spirit said you needed this."

His kind face looked at me with such sincerity and love, such conviction, an empathetic tenderness, as if he was seeing or feeling something I could not comprehend. He had a glimpse into the future, perhaps. I thought he felt a miracle was coming; we did all the right things. I was in control, doing two scans week by week, hospital stays, two surgeries, taking it day by day, month by month, to see my baby boys through an eight-month gestation period in the healthiest way possible. We had a very loving family to welcome them, and he came because he knew a risky miracle was about to happen. I was ready for it.

Shock

A few days later, I woke up, made a cup of tea, and kneeled over in massive pain. Not the kind of pain that was normal. Trembling, shaking, out of control. I couldn't breathe. Couldn't even speak. I started biting at my own skin, trying to ground myself in the pain. Paul had taken the kids to breakfast. He rushed home to find me on the floor, looking like I was seizing and doubled over in unbearable pain. He got me to the hospital in an ambulance, and my temperature was 105 and climbing. The infection was already winning, and I was going septic. I didn't have time to think; the pain blinded my mind from reality.

What I remember and what actually happened blur together like a bad dream, yet medical records don't lie when an infection spirals. There was no waiting. I was rushed straight into an emergency C-section under general anesthesia—fast, sudden, no warning. Just darkness.

"Septic. Shock. Hemorrhage risk." The words floated around Paul like they were smoke. I was far gone before he could say anything, swallowed by the sleep of anesthesia.

In the operating room, they worked fast. Myles came first. Then Sam. Sam cried right away, a sharp, clear healthy sound that cut through the sterile air. Myles didn't cry.

They whisked him to the corner of the room—doctors, nurses, wires, tubes, hands working fast and frantic. Quiet orders. No one looked up. When they were done, they wheeled him to a neonatal bed shoved in what was basically a closet.

What we didn't know, not then, was that Sam, in those last moments in the womb, had pumped nearly all his blood into Myles. All of it. Like his body was trying to save his brother.

But in the trying . . . Sam gave too much. Myles was already too far gone. And Sam was left almost empty.

The first doctor came to Paul quietly and said Sam had pulmonary hypertension. We knew that word. We hated that word. But Will had issues with it at birth and healed up beautifully.

I woke up slowly, heavy and cold, the world fuzzy at the edges. A nurse leaned close, whispering in my ear like she was telling a secret no one wanted to speak out loud. "You have an angel in heaven. And a beautiful son named Sam." I blinked, trying to pull her words into meaning, but the fog was thick.

Meanwhile, Paul was standing in two worlds, one foot with me, one foot with Sam—watching helplessly as the calls kept coming. The doctors were saying Sam needed a medi-flight. He was getting worse. Critical. His body was shutting down. "He lost too much blood at delivery," they told him. "He was still connected to Myles, too connected. When Sam pushed his blood over, he didn't get any back. By the time we realized it, it was too late." They pumped multiple transfusions into him. More. Then more. Trying to fill him up. Trying to save him. "Go rest," they told Paul. "We'll call you." But the call came too soon. His phone rang as he sat down beside me. The voice on the other end was tight, urgent.

"Come now." His stomach sunk. He quickly turned right around, flagged a taxi, breath caught in his throat. "Drive. To the hospital. My son's about to die."

When Paul stepped into the NICU that day, on the other side of London, they placed Sam into his arms. Small. Fragile. Still. And Sam—sweet, brave Sam—stayed alive for one more minute. Just long enough to die in his father's arms.

While I was under, floating somewhere between anesthesia and eternity, Paul was trying to hold six lives together, six hearts, six sets of needs with questions and fears. Three kids at home, two babies in crisis, and me, somewhere between this world and the next. He was making calls, talking to doctors, figuring out who to comfort, who to hand off, where to go, what to say. The man was running logistics on a level I hope no one ever has to. Meanwhile, I was gone.

When my body woke up, my soul didn't know where it landed. I opened my eyes; I wasn't sure if I was even alive. For a moment, I thought maybe this was the other side. Maybe I hadn't made it. Everything felt foggy, dark, and strange. My body felt wrong. My mind felt wrong. But somewhere under the fear was the quiet relief of being awake. Of still being here.

Like the aftermath of something massive. The drugs were still working their way out of my system, so reality came in pieces. The lights above me. The weight on my chest. The knowing—before anyone said anything—that everything had changed. Paul's face was in pain and love, and we held hands together. He was dealing with his own emotions on his sleeves.

His delivery had grace, showing his high EQ, through and through. He held me with his words, with his heart, and at that moment I remembered why I married him, how much I loved him. Not the wedding day kind of love. The in-the-trench-with-me kind. The I-will-break-with-you-but-not-before-I-carry-you kind.

It was soft and human. His voice didn't crack, but it bent under the weight of what he was carrying by the way he looked at me. I saw it all in his eyes. The sorrow, the reverence. The impossible task of telling your wife that your sons didn't make it.

It's not just the heart that breaks—it's the spirit.

The fear of any mom isn't just losing a child, it's losing herself in the process. Losing her mind, her grip, her voice, her strength. Losing that invisible thread that holds everything and everyone together. Then the unthinkable happens and the dread becomes reality.

I woke from surgery shaking so hard I thought my teeth would break. Couldn't stop. My whole body rattled against the hospital bed like loose change in a jar. The infection was still running wild in me, burning under the skin. And my incision. God, it looked like something out of *MASH**. Raw. Jagged. Ugly. A battlefield sewn shut.

I couldn't stop the shaking. But then I looked up.

And there they were. Oh, was my heart so thankful in this moment.

My two sisters and one of my best friends stood at the foot of the bed, faces pale and worried but smiling for me. And they were somehow here, somehow real in this strange London room.

And in that moment, still shaking, stitched up like a war survivor—I felt the strange mix of it all. Grief. Relief. Horror. Love. Life and death crashed together in this bright, sterile room.

But at least I wasn't alone. Not anymore. I felt such empathy for my youngest sister, with all that pain pouring off her sweet face. She stood there, helpless, her knowing eyes wide and wet, and I could feel the weight of it on her. She had been there through it all. Every hopeful text, every scary call. A cheerleader, coach, and advocate. Now, here we were. She couldn't fix it, nor could I. She looked so sad. It cracked something open in me.

My other sister? She was a lifeline in motion with my close friend Beth from Boston right beside her. Two angels in damage control mode. They didn't cry. They didn't flinch. They scattered like some quiet, invisible SWAT team, taking over my house while I lay wrecked in this hospital bed. Scooping up the kids, distracting them with trips to Harrods, buying treats, shiny bags of sweet things to make small faces smile. Keeping them away from the cracks in the world.

They folded laundry. They scrubbed the floors. They unpacked suitcases and ran the dishwasher and probably didn't even sit down. And my dog, Jackson? Peed all over their clothes, their bags, their shoes, like some furry chaos machine. They just smiled, wiped it up, and kept going. No sleep. No complaints.

They turned my house into a command center of clean, quiet, determined love. No orders spoken. No lists handed out. Just instinct. Just the old rhythm women know when things go dark: rise, move, save what you can. It felt like something out of *Little Women*. That old candle-light courage. When no one says what needs to be done because every-body already knows. Divide. Conquer. Fold. Clean. Feed. Protect. And they did. Everything without sleep. Without breaking. Because this is what women do when the world falls apart. They hold it. Quietly. Fiercely. For everyone else.

My oldest son, Ryan, was mature past his years, old enough to comprehend and feel the severity of the situation. The younger two, Grace and Will, not as strongly. My sisters and Beth were helpful in keeping the kids shielded from it.

There's not a way to explain the level of torture it is to look into your children's eyes who need you, attaching to your every word, strength, and mind and to tell them that despite picking names, plan-ning, praying, and giving them hope by looking full term, their brothers had died.

Not that the babies were gone—but those babies. The ones they talked to through my belly, the ones they felt kicking after dinner. The ones in the scan pictures taped to the fridge. The ones they were invested in, waiting, daydreaming. The ones their friends, classmates, and small community we had made were waiting on. It broke something in me, and whatever was left cracked again when I saw their faces trying to understand something that didn't make sense, not even to grown-ups.

We tried to comfort them, tried to say soft words like the pain would somehow land lighter, but nothing about it was soft. It was brutal. It was jagged. It was the moment that takes a childhood and slices a mark straight through it.

Neither Paul nor I had the tools nor prior experience holding a heartbreak to this degree. I immediately blamed myself and felt like it was all my fault. How could I not? A mother's job is to create, birth, and nurture. Her job is to protect her children. They grew in my uterus due to my choices, and it was my job to see both through to the end. Paul became even more of a task rabbit than he was before: do, move, work, and deal. I was the opposite. And then a small blessing came. In the middle of all that wreckage—fear, shock, pain—there was this one clear, unspeakably holy moment. We were all there. All eleven of us. My sisters. Beth. Father Stuart. My kids.

The living and the gone in the same room. A room so thick with sorrow and grace it almost hummed. Like the air itself knew to hold its breath. The boys were swaddled in soft white blankets and tiny, knitted caps were pulled gently over their perfect heads. They looked just like my older three when they were newborns. The same mouths. The same cheeks. Still and beautiful. So loved, wanted. So impossibly still. And we held them. Touched their soft faces. Their tiny fingers curled forever quiet. All of us, circling them with every ounce of love we had to give. It was birth and death in the same terrible, sacred breath. A beginning and an end folded into one trembling moment.

Father Stuart stood there, steady as a stone, his voice low and strong. Like a beam of comfort cutting through the ache. His words filled the room, not with answers but with faith. With something that could hold the weight of this without breaking.

For a moment, I wanted to go with him. Just leave this world, this aching body, and drift toward the peace in his voice. But I stayed. We all stayed.

The oil touched their skin, skin that would never bruise, knees that would never be scraped, never carry the weight of this hard life. Holy water wet their brows, water for boys who would never open their eyes. And in that breathless ceremony, they were welcomed into this world and released from it. Held. Blessed. Loved. The kind of holy moment you don't talk about in church because there aren't any words for it. It was a moment so sacred it almost shattered me to stand in it. But somehow, I did. We all did, and the room held us, quiet and full of God.

A safe, beautiful, worthy moment, like witnessing something so real your soul doesn't know quite where to put it because it matters. It wasn't abstract grief; it wasn't "loss." It was the boys we created in flesh, Myles and Sam. The boys we had two surgeries to save, dozens of doctor visits, scans, and hospital stays. The boys I risked my life and everything for. In that moment, they were seen, honored, and claimed by us, by God, by my sisters, Beth, our kids, and the universe itself. Not as a tragedy to sweep away and forget but as real lives. Moms who carry in their wombs for months and can't wait to meet, but this day, on August 9, my boys' hearts were not beating. It was deep, this feeling inside me that I couldn't protect them. I also couldn't give my living children the gift I created to give them, the end of a family chapter and the siblings they'd been waiting for. Everything failed. I failed.

When the nurses took Sam and Myles away, something broke inside me. Not loud. Not dramatic. Quieter than that. It was an empty, low ache that wrapped itself around my ribs and settled there. Heavy. Familiar. Like it planned to stay a while. Like it knew something I didn't. And in that quiet breaking, I looked at Father Stuart's kind, steady face—and thought, "Please, take me with you." I wanted to disappear into his world. Hide in a safe monastery. A quiet place where bells ring softly and no one asks you to smile, to be the leader, make dinner, or handle the weight of living in a foreign country with two kids starting a new school and another starting preschool. I wanted to go at that moment to a place where no one asks anything at all. I didn't want to go back to life at home. Not to the dog that peed on suitcases. Not to Paul's travel, work schedules, or to scraping together dinner or walking miles with no car. How was I going to function now? Who in the hell would want my company?

My world had just split in half. I didn't even want to be a person. I wanted to be air. A ghost. A spirit floating high above it all, where none of this could touch me. But my body—my poor, broken body—didn't care about any of that. It didn't care about timing or grief or loss or death.

It had its own plan. Even after the infection. Even after the emergency C-section. Even after all of it. Despite medication to stop it, the milk came in. My body didn't listen. The milk came anyway. My body thought there were two hungry babies waiting for me, and the cells screamed the question: Where are they? My brain knew where they were, knew they were gone, but my body didn't believe it. Knowing with your mind and knowing with your bones are not the same things.

My body only knew they were missing. I was a hands-on, skin-to-skin, baby-wearing, sit-on-the-floor, kiss-their-heads kind of mom.

The world expected me to move on; I couldn't. Because there was this haunting question in the quiet of every day: Where did they go? I needed to know. I needed to feel where my boys went. Not just believe. Not just hope. But feel it in my bones.

This is the part no one tells you about. The part after death, when grief turns into a pilgrimage. A long, slow walk with no map, no guide. Just a mother's soul forever searching.

I did everything I could to save them. Everything my body could manage, every prayer my heart could form. My flesh prepared for life even as my soul somehow knew the truth—they were already gone. And so, the questions came. Like quiet knocks in the middle of the night.

Do they have wings now? Are they still babies, or do they grow somewhere else—somewhere beyond this life? Who's holding them when I can't? Do they know they were loved? Really, truly loved? I read everything I could get my hands on. About heaven. About angels. About the afterlife. About what happens to babies when they leave too soon. I crammed for this like it was a final exam I never asked to take. Books piled on the nightstand. Articles saved. Podcasts. I researched. As if the right answer, the right verse, the right story, could make this mystery make sense. I didn't want closure. I wanted the truth. I wanted to find my boys. Even if it meant walking the edges of this world and the next, barefoot and bleeding, until I felt them. Until I knew. Maternal instinct doesn't know how to grieve. It just reaches to search. I couldn't stop looking for them in the air, in the hallways, in the blankets.

My head and heart were cracked so wide open, and my spirit drifted for such a long while. I wasn't fully here, and honestly, I didn't really want to be. Every day, I tried to be the best wife and mom I could. The three little faces must have felt my damaged goods. I went to the library every day, wandered into bookstores, scavenging. I was hunting for answers, for a map to the invisible.

I knew a boy had died in our home in Pelham Crescent before we moved in. I felt it, not in a scary way. In a real way, like energy still echoing off the walls. So I started to believe in things I'd never had to believe in before. Spirits. Angels. Presence. Mystery. Not just as metaphors or in church hymns but as real. As close.

What's strange is, where we were living at the time only added to this sense of something hovering just out of reach. Our house was in a crescent in South Kensington, London. Beautiful. Historic. Eerily quiet. I didn't know it at the time, but I was building a bridge between this life and whatever comes next. Maybe, just maybe, my boys were meeting me halfway.

The kind of reality you feel on the back of your neck. The kind of close that whispers when you're alone. I went to a different place, mentally and spiritually. An afterlife I didn't grow up knowing. A realm where my sons might still be somewhere, just away and out of reach.

I wasn't talking to dead people. I was just . . . listening. I was learning to be still with the mystery. I would pretend to be with them and envision us all together, and although my mind most days was my enemy, I also found it a little magical. I honestly became a woman I really didn't know, and it became truly comical in many ways.

3

THE DARK CAVE

In the days, weeks, and months that followed August 9, the dark cave became my new home. Everything I had ever feared in my adult existence as a mom had happened. Mind, body, and soul were gone. I hated myself so badly. I couldn't even see. I went down to the bottom floor, to a place I did not know the mind could even go to.

I will eternally feel the deepest empathy for any human being who goes here, who feels this kind of emotional darkness while trying on the brave face because they have no choice. I got accustomed to the dark; it wrapped around me like a heavy blanket—suffocating but familiar. When you feel naked with all your clothes on, when you're sitting in a room full of people and still feel like a ghost. When your world goes so dark it's just you, sitting in a black hole with no light, no rope, no exit signs—that's called fear.

The kind of fear that doesn't show up with fangs; it just sits on your chest and steals your breath. I was living inside of a fear I did not recognize, inside myself so deep, in a foreign country, alone. I didn't grieve; I just vanished. My soul went quiet. It didn't rage or weep—it simply fell asleep . . . like it couldn't bear to witness the weight of what had happened. I became a hollow version of myself, going through motions, floating through days I no longer recognized. I sat in churches with stained glass windows that used to bring me peace. I perched on park benches, watching mothers push strollers with babies I'd never hold. I boarded trains—moving trains—because sitting still was scarily unbearable. Trains filled with strangers with kind faces reminded me that humanity still existed, even when I felt like I no longer did.

Never a vanity queen, I gave up on pride. I had no strength nor the desire to even care. I gave up on hope, gave up trying. The job I loved the most in my whole heart was being a mom and a wife, and I could barely do that. I teetered right on the scary edge. The sunny days were the hardest, highlighting how dark I felt. I had to live in a pretend sitcom in my head, like, oh look, here I am! The lady who keeps losing babies but still remembers to put pants on! Had to adapt to the new strange, messed-up version of myself. I had to laugh at this "person" because I was absolutely pathetic compared to who I was just months prior.

I was hoping someone would come to knock on my door and say, "Ma'am, we've got a room for you (at the funny farm). Pack a toothbrush." And you'd just go. You'd honestly go because at least you wouldn't have to pretend anymore. There were no filters in the cave, no highlight reels, no affirmations, just you and your broken parts. The cave strips you; it exposes the bones of who you are, and from that place— where there's nothing left but breath—you begin.

That's exactly what happened to me when I never saw it coming. Many people research and travel to find this kind of cave to face their darkest fears and their own deliberate suffering. I was thrown into it with a shovel and no flashlight: fast, hard, and painful without the mental tools to do it.

There was a moment—sitting across from my husband, staring into his sweet, intuitive face—when I realized I was drowning, and I was pulling him under with me. I wanted to walk right out in front of that double-decker red bus and go away. He didn't say it outright. He didn't have to. He looked at me with such empathy, watching the woman he loved slip through his fingers. That's when he said, "Kate, I think you need to go to therapy." He made the call. He was the man that threw me a lifeline when I was too broken to ask for one.

Medication to help me? Truthfully, I was too afraid to get attached to a feeling I couldn't maintain on my own. I knew I had to feel it to get through it.

Despite this period of emptiness, my caring, loving, kind friends and neighbors offered help in a way that made me feel less like a burden and more like a person. And for a while those little things—they mattered. My angel friend was like a family, a neighbor; she mattered deeply. She had me over her house every single day after school for hours, but eventually, the world kept spinning and life kept living. People go back to their routines, and you're left alone, standing still, with a big fat, overstuffed suitcase of something that nobody else can carry.

My oldest two kids moved to a brand-new school in St. John's Wood, London, on August 18, 2008. It was called the American School of London. I stood in the parking lot, trying to look like any other mom who belonged when the reality sunk in. Today was the day that Sam and Myles were scheduled to be delivered. Yet, here I was in London, thousands of miles from home, C-section incision burning, hormones wild —sending my oldest two off for second and fourth grade. A few days later, my youngest son, Will, the baby again, the happiest, most dangerous distraction of all, started his first year of preschool at St. Nicholas Preparatory School, where the older two attended the year prior.

The first time I walked back into St. Nicholas after everything, I could feel the stares before the door even closed behind me. Little eyes were all watching. "Mrs. Santoro, where are the babies?" The question I knew would come. They saw me every day last year until mid-June. I wasn't ready for that question. I replied, "Oh honey, they're not here. They didn't quite make it." I spoke softly, as if that explained anything.

I thought, naïvely, stupidly, that this would be the day I'd finally stroll my two boys through Hyde Park. Two squirmy babies packed into a double stroller, me with a hot coffee, maybe bumping into another mom, maybe even smiling for once. But instead?

I bravely dropped Will off for his first day of preschool with a hollow chest and an incision that still burned under my jeans. Then I was just standing there. Dead alone.

That weird American mom in Hyde Park, the one whose belly was full-term and enormous, the one who lost both her babies. This was not me. Yes, but sadly, it was.

Nobody quite knew what to say. You could practically hear them whispering from the school office: "That's her. That poor thing." A flicker of a second. God help me—I actually thought: Yes, maybe I'll just push an empty stroller through the park today. Like a ghost. Like some sad, cracked woman pushing air. And I really almost laughed because I was tempted to do it. What the hell else was I supposed to do?

In Hyde Park, I had no plan, no boys, no babies. No friends. No framework to understand the current reality, just me and my busted body and the unbearable quiet. Yeah. That was super weird. Guess what? Grief makes you weird.

It turns Hyde Park into a graveyard and coffee into ashes, and there was no stroller to push.

My husband would scooter home from work just to check on me at lunch.

Oh, God. That was the total wake-up call. Imagine that. Miss Hold-It-All-Together being checked on like a patient?

Then he gently, too gently, suggested in a super caring, kind way: "Kate, maybe meds?"

I gave a look, a laugh, and not the graceful, polite kind of laugh. The tired, cracked, are-you-kidding-me kind.

Well, the next thing I knew, Paul was driving me to a psychiatrist.

Because clearly, Kate wasn't Kate anymore. I wasn't my happy-go-lucky, lively, smiling self. So, naturally, everyone figured a diagnosis and a prescription would patch me right up. Get her labeled. Get her sorted. Get her back.

And honestly? I was glad I went.

Because when the office door opened, out came this adorable British man, maybe five feet six on a tall day, with the kindest, gentlest, most reasonable face I'd seen in months. Like a real human who might actually see me. He sat down, smiled at me with that warm, patient look and said the words that cracked open the whole performance: "Kate, listen. There's absolutely nothing wrong with you." He let it hang there. Like oxygen. Like kind grace. "You really don't need any medication," he said softly. "You have been through a female war. But if your family wants a diagnosis—here, give them this one. Tell them you've got an adjustment disorder." He leaned in, smiling kindly, as if he was family. "Because you are, after all, a mom who is protecting everyone. You have just moved overseas to a brand-new city, into a new home, with a brand-new body, new environment, schools, pregnancy, new hospitals, surgeries. And you're grieving the loss of two newborn babies. You're sitting on a hormonal roller coaster strapped to expectations no one else can see. So what are you feeling? It's perfectly, painfully normal." And then, like the wise Brit he was, calm and clever, he gave me an option.

"If you want a script," he said, "I'll write you one. Might lift you up, help you peek above the clouds. No shame in that. But you don't need it. You seem like a soul who can do this."

Any intelligent person on the EQ side can see, feel, and know to always give a stubborn woman an option. And for the first time in a long time, I really felt seen. Not sick. Not broken. Just like a true human being.

He gently suggested talking it out with a woman in South Kensington and wrote me a script for six sessions. I chose to fill the prescription, but after three uneasy doses, I set it aside, knowing it wasn't the path I wanted to walk. I stayed. I stayed and slowly—so slowly—started learning how to sit with it. That suitcase didn't get any lighter. But somehow, my arms got stronger. Yes. That was the beginning of the raw, unfiltered, un-Instagrammable kind of grit I began developing.

I'm not wasting one more minute of this beautiful life.

4

DIGGING OUT

A full-blown peace exists and can live inside us all that doesn't need to be defended or explained. It can be found when you've lost it all and found you have a deeper appreciation for the gift of love that has been given to you, the miracle of just living.

When you've felt broken and rebuilt? You become truly unshakable. Like rock-solid unshakable, like you have superpowers.

I loved my kids and my husband with far more patience, more ease, more presence.

I became a better wife—faster to laugh, slower to complain.

From sheer and utter gratitude, from knowing I'd been given a second chance—and I wasn't wasting it.

This version of me? A gift.

I liked her a lot more.

She was softer, stronger, kinder.

She was home.

I remember sitting through our therapy sessions, mostly skeptical, arms folded in every way possible—literally, emotionally, spiritually.

I thought I could handle it all. That I should handle it all. I was in therapy across from a total stranger, explaining the kind of pain that doesn't even have words, and it felt a bit impossible, like I was speaking a language no one else could understand. I wanted answers, and if therapy couldn't bring them back, what was the point? Here's what no one tells you—grief, pain, and fear don't care how competent you are. They are not impressed by your stubbornness, by your to-do lists. They don't give a damn about your strong genes or health knowledge, nor how many fast times you ran the Boston Marathon. The real hard stuff, it just waits for you. In the silence. In the supermarket. In the middle of the night when you don't sleep while your body is still making milk for babies that aren't there, and no matter how strong you are, you will crack eventually. That six-week session of weekly therapy I did for Paul offered me a chair where I didn't have to pretend. It felt like work. Her empathetic face made me feel bad for her, which, in turn, made me feel worse.

Yet I'll give her this—she got one clean shot right before I walked out of that office for good. In that final session, she looked at me and said, "Kate, you seem like a sincere, caring friend. If a good friend of yours was in your circumstances, what would you do for them?"

I instinctually said, "Well, of course, I would go to the ends of the earth for that friend, never wanting them to experience anything like this. I'd do whatever possible to lessen the weight and offer them a moment of relief."

Boom. That was it. That's all she said. That ended it, no follow-up, just a goodbye. Clarity landed, just as I was walking out the door. So I left and started walking home, smelling diesel right near the South Ken tube station's flurry of busy. And damn, that question stuck to my ribs because I knew the answer.

I knew the kind of friend I'd be. The kind who shows up at the door with coffee, hugs, and silence. The kind who makes space for grief without trying to tidy it up. The kind who wouldn't dare say, "You pathetic soul, you should be doing better by now."

I'd never talked to anyone else the way I was talking to myself. She didn't cure me, but she opened that gift. I have talked more like that friend to myself ever since. Some days I fail, but at least now I know what I'm aiming for.

So when the stubborn person in me did what I thought was strong, to "stiff upper lip" my way through a season that no human should have to endure, I sank deeper in guilt and self-hatred. Those emotions became my roommates. They moved in and unpacked for six months. The world went dark, not the kind of dark where you turn off a light, but the kind where the sun could rise, and I still wouldn't see it.

I'm not saying tragedy is the only teacher, and, truthfully, I wish badly it weren't. Yet it was certainly mine. Adjustments can throw many of us off; roots keep us grounded. I liked the known, solid roots in life. Even as a young kid, I left notes on my bed to make myself feel better when I came back from a sleepover. The changes in a week's reality or a family trip threw me off. I felt alone, afraid of the dark, shadows, the wind, and certain scary men. I got so afraid of things even on TV, and everyone laughed and got a massive kick out of it because I was, as one would say, a "wimp" to a large degree, but I grew up and out of it. And when my husband lit up about a career-privileged move to London, I was so happy for him, and I followed.

That's the part of loving someone. Meeting them halfway, even when every part of you wants to stay put.

I never really wanted to go to London.

We had three healthy kids, a brand-new dream home, and flipped real estate four times as a side gig. We lived on the top of Beacon Hill across from Louisburg Square, a beauty of a home. I was just accepted into a dream program at the Institute of Medical Professionals at MG Hospital. I had our life map all stable, and this detour withdrew it.

London greeted us with low clouds, diesel in the air, and a daily gray drizzle that settled into my bones. There was a quiet melancholy. I didn't really know what it was that seemed to be missing until I sat on it for a while. Paul's career was moving forward fast, with fancy trips to other countries every weekend. None of this brought a fraction of the joy I felt when I looked at the small boy in his bright yellow raincoat and his two older siblings.

Will was a joyful firecracker, made the world feel lighter. He was my teacher in seeing the real magic in being a mom, the true joy that comes from what is standing in front of you. I was young enough and ready for one more. The bookend to the family chapter.

Having number three was the tipping point. We had the perfect boy-girl, two-kid family, which was great, but having Will opened my eyes to see where the true joy was—more of that! Less stuff, less money, less order. We had already walked through fears of an oldest son born with SVT. Then Will had pneumonia, pulmonary hypertension, and a collapsed lung. I could handle whatever was coming. I had handled it well before.

One of the emotions that helped grief the most was humor. My sister and I had a phrase we would use, walking into serious-toned events: "Let's keep it 'light and fluffy.'" So on bad days, I would have to revisit this.

The lady who lost the babies still shows up for snack duty. Yes, she hides behind trees in Hyde Park too! I used to hide behind a tree at Hyde Park just to see if my wild little son would even notice I was gone. Real healthy, I know. Parenting at its finest. Yes—grief makes you weird.

I'd duck behind the trunk of the thick trees like some pathetic soul, peeking out to watch him barrel around Hyde Park like a monkey. And then, bam—he'd stop, look around, wide-eyed, and burst into tears because he couldn't find me.

And there I was behind the tree crying too. What the hell was I doing? My new hobby, apparently, was playing hide and seek with sadness just to see if my heart was still working. Sad little games to keep the pulse going. You know . . . the normal mom stuff.

I've always hated roller coasters. Couldn't stand them. But there I was, suddenly the woman who'd ride any twisted, spinning, gut-flipping machine just to feel something. Anything. Like maybe if I let my stomach drop hard enough, my heart would remember how to beat without breaking. Turns out grief will make you line up for the stupidest rides just to borrow a little energy. Even if you scream the whole way down.

"If I were asked to give what I consider the single most useful bit of advice for all humanity, it would be this: Expect trouble as an inevitable part of life, and when it comes, hold your head high. Look it squarely in the eye, and say, 'I will be bigger than you. You cannot defeat me.' Then, repeat to yourself the most comforting words of all, 'This too will pass." —Ann Landers

5

QUESTIONS ASKED, MIRACLES ANSWERED

Grace isn't weak. True grace is what finally gave me the strength to face it all. To process it, to carry it, to own and be proud of it, to stop outrunning the pain and let it catch up to me . . . so I could walk beside it. That's the work. That's the climb and the quiet miracle. I didn't really understand what grace meant back then. I thought it was something we prayed on, said before dinner, and a form of being. A word tied to calm, gentle people—like my daughter, Grace.

But I wasn't really calm. I wasn't gentle. I was stubborn, strong, and more of a fighter type, not in a destructive way but an internal one. I was impatient. I was a mother of three who had just lost two children, and I was broken. How was someone like that supposed to feel grace? I'll never forget the day it began; it wasn't some grand awakening.

It was just another heavy gray day. I had been surviving, not living well, but something pulled me toward a stillness that day, and I found myself sitting back at St. Mary's church, arms wrapped around my body like a child, staring up at the wooden man on the cross, not because I was angry, but because it was time to go there. I felt still undeniably lost. I looked up, and I whispered, not shouted, "I'm not angry God, I am just numb, broken. I just don't understand. Why? Why see me go through the unknown to see me do everything I could, week in and out, up and down, medical torture, hope, fear, pray, to honor your code, to take both my boys back to you. Why? I wasn't trying to do anything more than to create two lives to love in your image to complete our family. I don't like to ask for more than I deserve, but I can't quite handle this sadness. Can you help me learn how to surrender? It feels weak, unnatural, and foreign, but maybe it's time now, God. Can you help guide me?"

That was the day the journey of grace began, not as a lightning bolt, not as an answer but as a quiet breath that somehow made it to my lungs, a soft presence that said, "You're still here." That was the start. That's the point I'm trying to get at: When I finally really surrendered, when I stopped fighting the dark and just sat in it, when I named the thing that was breaking me down and owned it without trying to polish it for someone else's comfort—that's when the real grace showed up for me.

My body felt weak, broken, bloated, and raw, like mangled meat. And my heart felt overused and beating from adrenaline—not the good kind either. I could laugh at this girl, a bird in a cage with blinders on flapping, panicking, completely disoriented. Yet—that dark cave? That became the very place where something beautiful cracked wide open.

That's where the transformation lives. Not in the perfect photo, not in the clean recovery. Not in the therapy room. It lives in the dark. In the moments where you want to crawl out of your own skin and disappear. It lives in the silence that makes you scream. It lives in that cave, where no one's coming and you have to figure out how to become the rescue you were waiting for. And I did. Not cleanly but with a little grit. With grace. With tears and with light because the dark didn't destroy me. It made me who I became.

You know that saying, "Nobody wants to build a home in a toxic body or a toxic soul"? Well, at that time, I had a little mix of both. For what felt like a very long time after everything I'd been through physically and emotionally—I was also told I probably couldn't have more children. Four C-sections. A body wrecked from infection. A thyroid that couldn't get its act together. An age they like to call "advanced maternal." At thirty-seven.

As I was sitting there again—laptop open, Google researcher, like some false prophet—searching angels in heaven. What happens to babies when they die? Adoption . . . surrogacy . . . sperm donors . . . frozen embryos . . . all of it like some insane late-night shopping spree for lost motherhood.

I wasn't really living. I was just digging. Trying to unearth some answer that would make it all okay. And then my sister would call. Like she did every day from America. Her voice—the only one that could cut through the fog, the only one that knew all the versions of me: the little girl me, the teenage me, the mother-me-now trying to crawl out of this hole.

"Kate. Come on. What are you doing?" She didn't tiptoe around it like everyone else in London did. "You can't sit there Googling angels and adoption and surrogacy and spirit babies and afterlife. What are you doing? You think this is the end? This isn't the end. You are young. You are whole. You are you. You don't end your story like this." She always knew where to jab the truth.

"Your doctors don't know you, Kate. They don't know the you who danced her face off at weddings or ran marathons with blood in her shoes. You are bigger than this. You are more than this. You don't quit here.

You keep going. You keep trying. You are worth what you want. And you have eggs, and you have parts.

And I'd sit there holding the phone, the silence of the flat pressing in, Hyde Park down the street, the empty stroller still folded in the hall closet. And for a minute—just a minute—I believed her. I wasn't done. I couldn't be. Hope was dangerous. But so was standing still.

The calls were everything. They were the intersection of impossible joy and unbearable fear, the whisper of faith meeting the roar of uncertainty.

You've walked us to the edge of a cliff, and now we see the courage it took to keep walking. This coaching was everything. An ultimate gift, just when you don't see it coming.

The gift always shows up just when you're least expecting it. When the experts have already closed the door, turned off the lights. I was sitting in a cold office in London at my OB/GYN follow-up. She looked me dead in the eye and said, "Be grateful you're alive, Kate. Take care of the children you have, adopt, or volunteer your time. Your chapter of carrying children is over." In my head, I thought: "Awe, lady, fuck you." What kind of sentence was that to someone with a pulse and a loving purpose?

This woman clearly didn't care, nor did she know me, a woman who would always find a way to make good on something bad, however it will be. The family chapter could not end in death and loss.

This "umph" can be a curse sometimes, but it's also the very same thing that's gotten me through everything. A gut-level knowing that this story isn't over. A light was back—dimly lit but back. I had not found a key for that door, but the switch was on. Grace doesn't float down like fairy dust. It rises from the fire. The grit you dig out of that grace? That's where the magic begins. I remember the exact moment it changed.

Coming home for Christmas that year was supposed to matter. For the kids. For tradition, for the family. And I tried—I really did. We had a little tree set up in a temporary rental right on the Boston Common. I strung some lights, hung a few ornaments. I attempted Christmas. But I wasn't ready to feel joy. Not fully. Not honestly. Pretending to be right took more energy than I had. So on that cold, beautiful Christmas night, snow falling soft and silence outside the window, I snuck away. I left the bustle of family and expectations and slipped off to a movie theater alone. I sat in the dark and watched *Marley & Me*, of all the damn movies. A story about loving and losing and letting go because apparently my subconscious wanted to bleed just a little more.

I wasn't quite looking for the light yet. Maybe a flicker. Maybe a shadow of it. But hope was still heavy. Everything felt like walking in mud—better, a little, but not free. What I really wanted was just silence. The comfort of shutting the world out for just one more night. When I finally made it home, back to the quiet apartment, the too-small tree, the snow still whispering against the windows—I went to change into my pajamas.

And that's when my husband glanced over and said, "Oh my God, Kate. Look at your boobs. The only way they could be that big is if you're pregnant." No, that felt sharp, dangerous, too fragile, and like walking barefoot over glass. Grief, I could wear it like a coat. But hope? Hope was a wide-open sky without a safety net. So I ignored him, laughed it off, and pretended not to hear him.

A few weeks later, my brother and his wife came to visit us in London. We were watching TV that night. I went to the bathroom, and it looked like a crime scene, blood everywhere.

The scary bad voices came right back. "You idiot, why and what are you doing? How much can you take, you weak fuck? Wake up and smell the coffee. It is not in your cards, so Kate, give up!" I was soaked in fear before I could even process what was happening. I took a sleeping pill that night, and the next morning, we went in for a D&C.

I lay there on the table, cold paper crinkling under me, staring up at the ceiling while the doctor prepped. This was supposed to be the beginning of the end—or the end of the beginning—I wasn't sure. But I barely let myself believe this was real. It was safer that way.

The room was dim. On purpose. He shut off the lights, flipped on the screen. The jelly hit my belly, cold as ice, and the wand moved slowly across my skin. And then . . . silence. A long silence. Long enough for my brain to think, is it cancer? Is it a cyst? A tumor? Something worse? Because he wasn't saying a thing. Just staring, frowning at the monitor, squinting. I turned my head, tried to stare at the wall.

And then he broke the silence, turning to me, reaching for my hand. His eyes were wide. His voice was soft. "Ma'am, I've got a heartbeat right here." I blinked. What?

"Oh—hold on, hold on. I've got two heartbeats. Look. See right here, ma'am? Two sacs. Two placentas. You're quite far along. Looks perfect. About eighteen, maybe twenty weeks." He smiled, gentle and proud, like he'd just found buried treasure. Like this was normal good news on a normal good day. Unexplained bleeding, that's all.

He didn't know me. He didn't know my story. The cave, my boys. The hospital rooms. The twin-to-twin transfusion. The fear baked into my bones.

No. To him I was just a woman—healthy, pregnant, with twins growing strong. Like this was happening to a person with a normal life. Two perfect sacs. Two perfect heartbeats.

Like some quiet miracle slipped in while I wasn't looking. And for the first time in months, I breathed.

Let that sink in. My husband and I both were well. There were no words to describe it. We were a little in shock, driving in the car that day on the opposite side of the road toward home, feeling like we had no words to say to one another. Total and divine grace. We were like Mr. and Mrs. Claus with two huge bags of gifts that just jumped into our spirits and laps. They were bags so magical and meaningful with a love so deep that words aren't worthy of any of it.

When the door closes, I find a window. When the window locks, I kick in the side gate. If the track is closed, I climb the fence. All I knew at that moment was this: how to persevere.

The coping mechanism was simple and strategic.

Don't speak it into existence; just carry on. Don't scare the kids or the dozens of caring, drained people who walked through it with us.

If we didn't say it out loud, maybe it wouldn't be real. If it wasn't real, maybe I wouldn't have to watch another heartbreak unfold. So I kept it quiet and heard the term "cautiously optimistic" way too many times. Nobody in our lives knew we were having twins, not because we wanted a surprise—but because we didn't want to worry anyone. All the way to thirty-eight weeks. Full term. Two healthy baby girls. And it wasn't until they were about five years old that I let myself fully believe they were staying. That they were mine. That they were safe.

Some people wish for that one college acceptance. Some people wish for billions. Some wish for better health, wealth, for the one job. The girl, the man, the partner, the diagnosis, the dream team.

For me back then, it was just wishing to be myself again. The one feeling I took fully for granted was the simple comfort and luxury of just being myself.

Who you are matters.

If you feel off, depressed, anxious or stuck, whatever and however the feeling of fog or lack of clarity looks like for you, whatever shape your deepest hopes and darkest moment takes from you, please feel this.

I vowed to myself fifteen years ago that I would share this story because I just wanted to find a book in a bookstore, one that spoke enough to me to know and feel with certainty that I was going to heal, not just back to myself but even better. I didn't think I was, and I never read or found the book I needed back then, so I decided to write this book for you to know that you will too.

So Keep Going

To anyone reading this—I truly hope you see that I'm living proof. This fight, this series of unforeseeable, hard challenges—you can thrive through it.

You can be content. Happy. Even surprised and amazed by what's still coming.

So you keep going on that journey, OK? Even when you feel like shit.

Especially then. Just keep going.

I hope and believe and know with all my heart you will get there, just like I did. Because sometimes, dreams do land.

And when they do—they're five times what you imagined and stronger than anything you thought you could build.

Through the "can't," "shouldn't," and "never will," could it be? Hell yes, it could be because life doesn't always knock. Sometimes it just kicks the damn door in. Wham, bam. Thank you, ma'am.

That was the year I found out who my real friends were. Not the "Let's get coffee sometime" crowd. The real ones, the ones who barely knew me but showed up anyway. I'm talking about a group of moms who organized six months of meals every single night.

Divine intervention delivered in Tupperware. Casseroles with halos. Kindness wrapped in foil. And the house, absolute chaos, beautiful, hilarious chaos. My daughter decided bangs were her destiny, grabbed the scissors and gave herself a haircut. Fine by me, my little Willy Wonka. A Nutella-drenched maniac. Climbing furniture, laughing like a lunatic, leaving chocolate fingerprints on everything except the ceiling —and I'm still not totally sure about the ceiling. Meanwhile, my oldest son? That kid turned into a rock, brave, kind, caring, intuitive, and responsible. He was the shield for the younger two during it all; he was mature enough to see it older than his years. He was quite strong in a way that made me ache and admire him at the same time. He'd read fifty-seven books on the tube that year. Back and forth to school, burying himself in pages, building a world no one could touch—because the one around him had gotten too damn loud.

We had a puppy that chewed through half our life. The house was never clean. Toys were strewn through every room. The laundry deserved its own zip code. Knowing what came so often toward me was like the gut punch: four days after losing Sam and Myles, it was Ryan's birthday. I have that mental picture framed. Then nine days after walking into their new school, smiling at teachers, nodding like everything was fine, and pretending I wasn't untethered inside. I had to hold it together and wear the mask of a mother while I felt like a puddle of grief and grit.

This is the moment when you learn who your kids truly are and how much they love you. That's when you find out. Not when things are easy, but when life sucker-punches you and hands you a clipboard and says, "Sign here, smile, and keep going." That's when the true ones show up. Not with words. Not with pity. Sometimes, it shows up in your son's kind smile, a warm meal, a bus driver, sincere friend, or in a flower in Hyde Park that reminds you that you're still alive.

An awakening didn't come with trumpets or choirs. It came in subtle shifts. What happened next wasn't a miracle. It was a slow reintroduction. To myself. To my faith. To a God I didn't need to understand to feel. I had started to awaken, not away from the pain but through it. And on the way, I started breathing a little easier in the strength I didn't know I still had. In a sense, it felt as if I was being carried—not by answers, but by presence. In realizing that grace doesn't always arrive dressed in robes.

The worry was real. How was this fragile body supposed to give twice the blood after losing so much, after the risk of hemorrhaging, carrying twice the life again? That same blood that had stopped flowing for two tiny souls I never got to take home? My C-section incision had just healed, and my stomach was stretching again, not logically nor safely. It felt like standing on a high wire, arms out, knees shaking, looking down at that canyon of grief.

This two-year period, 2008–2010, was by far the bravest time of my life, not because I didn't feel fear, but because I let the fear walk right beside me, and I didn't run. It wasn't a clean kind of brave. It was messy. A mix of white-knuckling the moment and whispering to God, "You better know what the hell you're doing because I sure don't." Something inside me—call it a flicker, call it divine, call it mother's instinct—said, "Stay the course. You're made for this."

I can see now that you don't earn grace. It's not easy to recognize it, but when it shows up, it carries you over the tightrope, whether your knees are strong or shaking.

I started healing. Not just physically but in the deep places. The unexplainable spaces, the ones you can't see in scans. The ones where bitterness lives, where fear camps out, where heartbreak used to have its arms crossed and feet up on the table.

Two lives finding home in a body that was told no and a soul that had finally said yes.

Looking back, it's no wonder the girls chose to come then. They made a home inside a woman who was finally becoming a home to herself.

Not perfect, not fully fixed but safe, soft, peaceful, and open. That's the part they don't tell you: sometimes healing doesn't look like kale smoothies or green juice with yoga; sometimes, it looks like crying in the park, forgiving whatever it was that hurt you. Talking to yourself in a way you never did before. Slowing down.

Taking a walk in the rain when you don't feel like it. Letting hope sneak in.

Those girls were my miracles, but the real miracle started the day I stopped fighting the darkness and began turning on the light by choice.

It was a full-circle moment, the way joy can return, not just to you but through you and your whole family. Here's the thing no one tells you about grit: anyone can develop it. It doesn't come back in some big dramatic blaze. It rebuilds like sand in an hourglass. Tiny, imperceptible grain. One day, I'd feel just a flicker. A single spark.

The appreciation for that flicker was bigger than winning a lottery ticket. Then I'd get nothing for a week. Then another grain—one warm moment, one smile, one walk, one tiny accomplishment that no one else would see as anything important.

But to me, it was gold, and over time heat became warmth, warmth became power, and power became grace.

It was slow, so painfully slow it was maddening, but the fire started to change. It morphed—not into rage or hustle or denial but into something warmer, softer, and more peaceful. It morphed into moments of grace. And let me tell you—grace isn't weak.

Grace is what finally gave me the strength to face it all.

To process it. To carry it. To stop outrunning the pain and let it catch up to me so I could walk beside it. That's the work. That's the climb. That's the quiet miracle.

So eventually, I didn't just crawl out of the cave. I flew out of it.

I had spent much of my life avoiding the kind of love that could break me, thinking it would make me weak. But it didn't. It remade me into someone real. Someone raw. Someone capable of looking pain straight in the face and still choosing to love deeper. Live louder. Serve more quietly. And walk—barefoot, broken, and wide awake—into grace.

"Everything we shut our eyes to, everything we run away from, everything we deny, denigrate or despise serves to defeat us in the end, what seems nasty, painful evil, can become a source of beauty, joy and strength, if faced with an open mind." —Henry Miller

6

BACK TO BEANTOWN: A REBIRTH

"Serendipity. Look for something, find something else, and realize that what you've found is more suited to your needs than what you thought you were looking for." —Lawrence Block

The housing market suddenly collapsed. Paul thought ahead, and he made the call to go back to America. He was a ninja master at masking his stress. It happened quite fast.

Two weeks from the moment he made the call, the wheels touched down in Boston. Just like that. Paul moved quickly. Like a man on a mission. Like a man who knew the weight of what was riding on the decision and wasn't going to waste a minute. Me? I was slower. Everything looked different now; I was not the same person who left Boston, but I liked this person better now.

I walked through those days like they were thick with grace, fear, a little hope, yet stitched with grief. My body was swelling with the weight of the twins. My heart was swelling with the weight of everything else. I was twenty-eight weeks to the day when the plane landed in Beantown.

Literally and metaphorically. The place where my story had started. And somehow, here I was again. Our old house? Sold. Our life? In storage—box after box of the life we'd built overseas.

Memories were wrapped in newspaper and bubble wrap, waiting for the next chapter. Paul is a man with a list and a timeline and just enough to make it happen. When I walked into what was going to be our new home, a three-bedroom apartment, I could have cried. It didn't matter that it wasn't fancy. Or big. Or forever. It was organized. Set up. Done.

No more takeoffs. No more airports. No more accents and confusion and wondering which direction the cars were coming from. We had a car, and I could drive. An American minivan car. In a garage. I stood there in the quiet of that apartment and felt something I hadn't in a long, long time. Home.

Maybe not the house. Maybe not the perfect plan. But home. And for the first time in two years, I breathed a sigh of relief. I was thrilled.

At about thirty-four weeks' gestation, life handed us another speed bump. Paul was traveling on a work trip. Ryan had this really bad cough; something about it just didn't sit right. He looked pale to me. Off. I begged the team at Mass General for a chest X-ray. Begged because I had that quiet, knowing gut feeling that only a mother gets. Sure enough, as we pulled out of the parking lot on the way to the golf course, the cardiologist called me directly. Her voice was calm but serious. Ryan's heart was enlarged, there was fluid where it shouldn't be, and his heart rate was dangerously low. Extremely dangerous.

"Turn around," she said. "Please come back now."

I did. I played it calmly, walked right back into that hospital, looked the doctor straight in the eye and said, as smooth as I could, "I can handle just about anything, but today, you will do everything in your hands to ensure my sweet healthy son is going to be okay. Doc, I've been through hell and back. Please, can we admit him right now? Put that pacemaker in."

She felt me; she did exactly what I asked. Ryan handled that one like he was Ironman with a battery. Irish folks have weak hearts, I guess.

August 25, 2009

The scheduled C-section day came. I climbed into the car, belly stretched tight as a drum, and for the first time in months, maybe since London, a thin, cautious thread of real hope slipped in beside me.

Maybe. Maybe this time it could work. I couldn't let it in all the way, of course. Just the edge. Just an inch. Because the rest of me was still locked in that old, familiar place—PTSD on a low simmer, denial wrapped tight around my heart like gauze. Another hospital. Another operating room. But this time, it was America. Boston. Mass General. Not King's College. Different doctors. Different accents. Different air. MGH was where Ryan, Grace, and Will had been born.

I lay down on the cold operating table, blinking up at bright lights, the blue sheet rising across my chest. The sterile smell. The hum of machines. It all felt like a movie I'd seen before—too many times. Only this time, I wasn't sure if I was playing the lead or just some extra passing through the scene. Trusting but not trusting. Believing but holding my breath. Maybe they're ready. Maybe they'll come out breathing. Maybe this time it'll be different. But no matter how hard I tried, the old fear curled in the corners of my mind a little like smoke. Because I'd smelled it and had been here before. And I knew what could happen, especially being "advanced maternal age with history."

So I stayed half in, half out between a little belief and a lot of self-protection, waiting for the next chapter to write itself.

And then—before I could gather another thought—there it was. A cry. Then another. Sharp and strong. Two healthy, beautiful cries cutting through the air like light breaking into darkness. Two of them. The whole thing, as Ryan says. The whole thing.

Alive. Fully alive. Big, pink, perfect girls—each just six pounds of fierce, squirming life. It wasn't a birth. It was a true resurrection.

A rising from the grave of what had been lost. A moment of awe.

There are no words for what it felt like to see them. Two perfect little lives. Lying there like tiny little dolls, only real, impossibly real—right in front of me, as if they'd slipped gently from heaven to earth while I wasn't looking.

I stared at them, stunned, feeling something so deep it didn't even have a name.

Joy, grace, humility, and holiness. Something sacred. Something that made me want to fall to my knees right there on the hospital floor and weep.

I kept thinking: Did this actually happen? How could I, of all people, feeling a bit cracked, wrecked, and grieving, be given this beautiful gift?

Not one but two fierce, perfect girls. After everything. After London, moving internationally back and forth. After hope, prayers, then loss. After feeling fear so thick, I'd forgotten what hope even felt like. It was all too surreal. It was beautiful. Too full. I felt exactly like the man in that scene in *The Blind Side*, when the boy holds something precious in his big hands and you can see it on his face—the weight, the wonder, the quiet shock of holding life itself. That was me. Holding this moment. Full. Silent. Wide-eyed. My heart cracked open so wide that God himself must've slipped in. When the joy is that big and impossible, your system can't even handle it, and the world slows down. Every breath taken from that day forward has felt like borrowed magic.

From that day till today, everything in my life has looked like a series of miracles with sprinkles of magic.

I hadn't even fully wrapped my head around the fact that these two babies were actually going to arrive. Like, really arrive. Breathing, crying, real little humans. It wasn't just my day; it was everyone's day. My husband, our three children, my parents, my sisters, brothers, Beth, Miranda, and Remy. I had so many wonderful souls rooting for me. Seeing the faces of Grace and Ryan—they felt this moment as much as I did, and they glowed with a moonbeam of satisfaction.

My in-laws still had no idea we were carrying twins. My mother-in-law kept saying everyone was confused, traumatized, talking about twins.

We hadn't even dared to buy cribs. Not after everything. There was one old pack 'n play shoved into the corner of our three-bedroom apartment—all 1,500 square feet of it—like we were trying to sneak these babies into life without waking fate itself.

When life hands you that kind of grace, the rare, trembling kind—you don't dare expect more. You make do. You pray. You stay small and quiet and grateful as hell.

My Grace, sweet, gentle Gracie, became grace in human form. Something shifted in her. Like the universe slipped her a quiet little note that said, "It's your turn to grow up now, kid." And boy, did she listen. She had slipped back into her old elementary school to third grade like she'd never left, steady as a stone. Turned into the teacher's pet, not in the loud, hand-waving way—but quiet, kind, calm. A little leader no one saw coming.

Her schoolwork was perfect. Her confidence bloomed like something secret and slow. She navigated that world all by herself, graceful and sharp, patient and sure. A little fairy of quiet courage. We watched as she grew up before our eyes. Mornings were a quiet sort of circus.

I'd be sitting on the couch, trying to nurse both girls at once, one tucked under each arm like little footballs, while Grace hovered nearby, just out of reach, watching with those big eyes that had already seen too much. She understood. In that way kids sometimes do when life demands it too soon. Without words, without explanation, a part of her knew.

Same with Ryan.

Both felt the weight of what had happened—the loss, the shift, the silent responsibility hanging in the corners of the house. And they carried it with a kind of grace that made me smile. All heart. No fussing. No tantrums. Just gentle, quiet help.

Grace would straighten the blankets, fetch a burp cloth, and bring me a bottle without being asked. Little hands trying so hard to keep up with life's big tasks. Sometimes, she'd stand there, backpack on, hair brushed, and ready for school. She'd look at me with this serious face and say, "Mom, what if I just stayed home today to help with the girls?" Like she was nine going on forty. A little old soul in footie pajamas.

I'd smile, swallow the lump in my throat, and tell her no, school was her job. But oh, part of me wanted to say yes, and many days I did. Or she was a few minutes late to school so I could enjoy those mornings with her.

She had an education by letting her stay in the safe circle of home, where we were all bringing joy, life, and things back together.

Ryan—our little man. That's what we have always called him because that's exactly what he was. A tiny grown-up in disguise, like someone shrank down a businessman and sent him off to school in a suit and tie with a brand-new device in his chest.

He was only eleven years old when life got flipped upside down, and somehow, eleven years old by the time he hit fifth grade. Growing up way faster than he should've, carrying more than any little boy should have to but handling it all with quiet strength, even when it wasn't easy.

Because that's who he was. Our little man, figuring it out as he went. The kids felt the joy in their own bones—a joy and the feeling of indescribable love. Willie was a true daily comedy, a fun one. They all became like three little magical nannies overnight, mini mommies and daddies in training—ready with burp cloths, bottles, and fun.

Ryan was more than a son; he was the flagpole of our family. I had Ryan when I was just twenty-six, and looking back, I realize he shaped my parenting more than anyone else ever could. Born with this wild sparkle in his eye and a firecracker grin, he had an enthusiasm for life that made everything feel big and bright. He was very smart and had a strong personality and presence. Even as an infant, he was perceptive, sharp, and very fun to have as my firstborn. He kept me on my toes, taught me how to move fast, think fast, live fast. It was me and him against the world in those early years, two connected souls figuring it all out as we went. Paul would travel half the month, so Ryan came with me to work; he came with me everywhere.

Ryan was and still is the pulse of our family. He developed the endurance I created from day one. Every museum, every baseball field, every soccer game—we did it all. I even dragged him to the squash courts just to keep him busy, tossing balls around for hours every day, packing a backpack full of bats, clubs, balls, anything he could swing or throw. From the time he could walk, he was doing the whole thing—hitting, throwing, running—what he called "the whole ting." He was the spark, the energy, the heartbeat in the middle of all of us. He made me a mom.

Ryan was brave through it all, especially in London, when life threw more at him than any kid should ever have to carry. But he never let it weigh him down. Always forward-thinking, always communicating clearly, like he somehow knew even back then how to handle life's sharp edges with grace.

Even after all the heart surgeries, you'd never guess—not in a million years—that he'd ever faced a setback.

Our apartment became a home again. Those days were, hands down, the happiest days. Not because they erased the pain but because they validated it. Those times are joy, yes, but more than that, they are my proof. The reminder to keep moving forward no matter what. Once they were old enough to walk, just shy of a year, I laced up my sneakers again. This time, I wasn't running away from pain; I was running with peace. Running as someone reborn. Running as a woman who had come back from the edge and brought back a whole new self with her.

7

LACING UP AND LEANING IN

"Be a rainbow in someone else's cloud." —Maya Angelou

The following year, I got this casual little tap on the back from a girlfriend at church. "Hey, Kate, want to run the Boston Marathon with me this year?"

I sort of laughed out loud. I had one baby on each hip, my boobs were in two different time zones, and I hadn't seen my abs or done cardio or strength training in quite a long time. So physical fitness? I needed a nudge.

Yes, but right there? That's the power of a buddy, a sincere girlfriend, a mom with the same goals. One little nudge, and suddenly, the thought doesn't sound so crazy. Suddenly, you remember you've got sneakers in the closet and something still burning in the tank. So I said yes. And soon enough, I got us two bibs for the Michael Carter Lisnow Respite Center, "Michael's Miracle," an official BAA charity partner.

Every dollar raised by their marathon team goes toward respite care —short-term relief—for families of children and adults with developmental disabilities. Their fundraising has underwritten hundreds of thousands of hours of free or subsidized care.

For the record, the only true test of athleticism I've ever cared about

—hands down, no contest—was carrying two sets of twins, back-to-back.

Five cesarean sections—and carrying Lucy and Riley—basically built me a second torso. I had massive varicose veins bulging out of the backs of my legs, thick and angry like highways. My body didn't feel remotely worthy of doing anything like running—mostly because I didn't have the time or the energy. Honestly, this would've been the perfect moment to hang up my running shoes for good. Switch to yoga, Pilates, a little weight training, and ride off into the sunset of mom mode. Yet when that friend tapped me on the shoulder? Something old woke up, and something new stepped forward too.

My good friend had a deep love and respect for Boston—its history, its running legacy, and especially Patriots' Day, April 15—when the Boston Marathon turns the whole city into magic. The most epic day of the year.

Getting a bib and raising a good chunk of money while committing to a full training schedule with two babies and three budding middle schoolers was no small order. It was a big commitment. My running partner was the plus to my battery. We were a bit of an odd couple. She was steady, strong, always ahead of schedule. Organized to the core. She loved data—splits, spreadsheets, results, you name it. She liked the numbers. Me? I just liked running. The freedom. No watch, no set pace, no real plan. Just movement and breath. She kept us on track; I kept us light. And that balance? It mattered. Because let's be honest—training for a marathon with five kids is basically a full-blown comedy act. And somehow, between her structure and my chaos, we made it work.

Nursing, wall sits, foam rolling, taking work calls—and dropping the phone on your baby's head. Reheating the same cup of coffee for the third time. Making four other meals. No time to shower. Every second of the day, you're on demand.

You wanna know how to get out of your damn head with a shitload on your plate? Put down the iPhone, the guilt, the to-do lists, and pick up your sneakers, or whatever your own damn passion is, and set a goal for yourself . . . and do it.

After more than a decade of carrying lives, my brain felt like scrambled eggs, and my body and spirit were starving. A lot of caregiving, moving, parenting, baby-making, body-breaking, identity-shaking years. Ten years of burp cloth, breast pumps, cross-country identity whiplash, heart surgeries.

This is the kind of emotional mileage that doesn't show up on a Garmin, but it burns just the same.

And then one day, through all that noise—I heard it.

There was a voice inside me. Not the mom voice. Not the polite wife voice. Not the friend voice.

The other one. The deep one.

The quiet one.

The one that cuts through all the noise—you shouldn't, you're not supposed to, you can't, you've put on too much weight, you're too skinny—kind of noise.

No. This voice was the badass voice.

And that voice was so loud. So strong. So damn determined.

It said: Lace up, KJ. We're going for a good, long, strong run.

Because here's the thing: When you're about forty, you're not even close to done.

Even if you're hiding your running shoes from your toddlers—who think they're treasure chests. The other one. The deep one. The badass one that had gone quiet in all the noise of "should" and "supposed to."

She and I would roll out of bed at 5:00 a.m., half-awake, and drive to races all over Massachusetts—swapping kid stories, catching up on life, laughing about the chaos.

I'd always forget something. She'd always remember everything.

We did this dozens and dozens of times, season after season. And these weren't just runs. They were little rebellions. Little escapes. Just for us.

Four miles to Harvard. Four laps around the track.

Four miles back. Year after year—the loop around the Charles River.

Every step. Every inch. Every person we knew.

My hair? I went so long without brushing it, it basically staged a protest. Matted, tangled, dreadlocked itself into one giant knot I proudly called a ponytail. And no—I didn't bother to brush it. Didn't care. I'd just pop up and go.

She'd take one look at me and laugh every time.

I wasn't chasing fancy sneakers the experts said were best. Some days I was racing down a path, dreadlock ponytail not flying, ripped clothes, shoes from God knows when, not a care in the world. I didn't care how I looked or even smelled.

A joyful, happy hippie on the move, no makeup, no maintenance. It was me, and I liked it that way.

When you've watched yourself break and come back to life, the last thing that matters is the matching set from Lululemon. What matters is that you're moving. What matters is the wind in your ears, the dirt on your calves, the breath in your lungs, the feeling of sheer aliveness pulsing through your chest like some ancient rhythm that never died and just waited for you to remember. That is what my everyday runs felt like.

Nobody in the real world could even relate to them.

8

FOOTFALLS AND FRIENDSHIP

Every morning at 8 a.m., I'd drop my daughter Grace off at school, then meet my girlfriend on the corner. We'd run. The air was crisp. Twinkles danced on the water. We'd pass the tree along the Charles River where we sprinkled Sam and Myles' ashes— sitting right at the edge, we'd watch that tree change year after year.

The Charles River became sacred ground—a moving session of social sneakers, sweat, and life. In that rhythm, I saw something holy. Growth.

If it was zero degrees or below, we ran. No excuses.

And my attire? Definitely a joke.

I basically got laughed at every single day for what I showed up wearing.

My run pal was of good character; she knew and respected the pain I shouldered, making me feel stronger for it. Whatever was said on that road stayed on that road.

That pavement? It will remember things no one else ever will. It holds the weight of so many stories, like a journal that never judges. There was a tribe of us. I was definitely the weak link, back of the pack —no shame in that—but I had a fire in my belly. It didn't have a direction, but it was there.

The right group of women, all in it for the same goal.

This crew—we got wings together.

They didn't just show up—they helped carry me along.

We all had busy lives, tired eyes, full workloads, but no matter what, we'd lace up and move together.

Running toward strength—whatever kind we needed—on any given day, month, or season of our lives.

Now, I wasn't entirely sure what decade it was, what time it was, how to use a watch, or do mile training effectively, but I really did not care.

Those days of 2012 to 2022 running around that majestic Charles River are tattooed in my memory, etched in the kind of way that doesn't fade. Every step, every mile marker, every conversation that unfolded beside me were like prayers on the move.

Snow. Sleet. Rain. Humidity. Heat.

That loop became a second home. A sanctuary. A church pew and a dance floor. Those years—those runs—they are right up there with the best memories I will ever have.

The Charles River didn't just see me run, it watched me become.

People always asked how I fit marathon training into seven schedules, two babies, a full house, and a traveling husband working so hard to provide. And honestly? The answer was simple: the power of a running buddy. None of the races, the miles, or the memories from the past decade would've meant half as much without her by my side. She made the miles matter.

For me to get it done, I learned the fine art of being wildly creative on the fly. Training plans, yeah, they are cute in theory, but survival mode writes its own workouts.

There's nothing convenient about stolen training moments. And trust me—they were anything but glamorous. They looked like this: Throw two kids into the double jogger and push it uphill with groceries stuffed underneath like a cart full of bricks. Or run sprints up hills while flipping pages of a book and singing out loud just to keep the kids entertained. Sometimes, I'd drag them to a grass field and run the bases with them—pretending to be the substitute baseball, soccer, lacrosse, or track coach—anything to keep them moving while I squeezed in training. Whatever it took. Make it a game. Make it count. Get the miles in. Somehow. I can remember trying to sing to them while pulling that crinkly plastic shield over the double jogger, making sure nobody got cold or windblasted. It was like pushing a rolling greenhouse with snacks and small humans inside. Sometimes, the jogger would tip sideways. My wrists felt like they were going to crack, juice boxes were flying, kids' shoes had flung off somewhere behind us, and wind was whipping in our faces. But Mom had to get her run in.

And they just came along for the ride. The crazy part? They actually liked it.

On a busy weekend, I'd pack the running shoes, get dumped off on the highway halfway home. Paul would say, "You gotta get your long run in," and just drop me on the side of the road—maybe twenty miles from home if we were coming back from a soccer game or somebody's birthday party.

Sometimes that just meant running the rest of the way back.

No big deal. Just another day, another adventure in marathon training.

For five years we'd take the kids up to Vermont every weekend to ski. I'd run in sneakers through two feet of cold snow or hike in ski boots at zero degrees, climbing up the mountain like some frozen pack mule.

Or I'd run alongside the car in traffic, racing Paul just to keep the kids laughing.

A little strange? Sure. But I got it done.

My running buddy wilts like a flower in heat and does not sleep. We had completely opposite challenges. I was running without any iron in my system and didn't know it. She was running without proper recovery and sleep.

She was the GPS when I got lost, which could happen in races.

It takes a certain kind of friend as an adult who knows you well enough to remind you of the things you will forget, like signing up for things on time or remembering to take creatine right after a run.

We ran our first Boston together in our late thirties, then the California International Marathon twice. And together—against all odds—two back-to-back fast marathons—we both qualified for the World Championship Marathon Majors in London.

Bring the kids along?

We crammed five kids in one hotel room, with two babies sharing a crib that we wheeled into the bathroom like it was a mobile nursery unit because when you're running the New York City Marathon and you're also a parent, space isn't a luxury, it's just a suggestion.

Marathon race mornings? We were up at 4 a.m. for many races around the country, trying to pull off a covert operation, pinning bibs in the dark, sports bra acrobatics in total silence, tiptoeing around bottles, dirty socks, and diapers like landmines. I crept into tiny hotel bathrooms like a Navy SEAL, only to find my race-day reflection. The babies were asleep two feet away in the bathtub crib, and my biggest fear wasn't the 26.2 miles ahead—it was waking them up.

I didn't disappear into motherhood. I expanded.

Every mile was a reminder that I still had grit—and now, far more peace and grace.

Looking back now, I'm thankful for every single mile, slow, fast, painful, bloody old shoes and all.

They're mine; nobody gets to take them away.

Not the noise, not the critics, not even the years that tried to tell me I was too tired, too old, too injured, and too mommed out to do something wild again.

There's something wild and instinctual that kicks in after a hard time in grief as the gun goes off at the start line of any race that says, "Time's running out—giddy up, girl." At forty, I felt that fire.

Over time, my heat became warmth, warmth became power, and power became grace. It was slow. So painfully slow it was maddening.

This became a powerful emotional beat in my life, and I had no idea what was coming.

Just a few years ago—before the grace, before the flickers of warmth —I remember my mother-in-law saying to me: "Kate, grief is a process. You can't rush it." God, I hated and resented that comment so badly.

I didn't want to hear that. I didn't want to feel it. What I wanted was to fix it. A fast-forward button. I wanted to skip the whole damn thing and run it down. But once I was neck-deep in it, living it day by day, hour by hour—I knew she was right. You can't rush grief. You can't outwit it. You can't walk through it without scars. You can't dance around it in your cute shoes and think it'll just move along. You carry it. You earn your way through it, and somewhere in that unbearable middle, something shifts. Something real.

Something good.

9

THE BOSTON MARATHON BOMBING, 2013: WHEN THE WORLD STOPS RUNNING

Running through the finish line that day, smelling like salt and exhaustion, I grabbed a medal and found myself lying on a cot in the medical tent getting ice. I was lying on a cot to stretch when it happened. At first, it sounded like a loud firecracker, except sharper and deeper somehow. Then another loud pop. The strange, thick smell of smoke. Papers flew everywhere right outside the tent window. The medical tent at the finish line shifted in an instant, one moment tending to tired, cramping runners gulping water, rubbing sore legs, and the next, it was sheer chaos, becoming an emergency room for the suffering bombing victims. In a matter of seconds, the whole purpose of the place changed. Finishing medals and electrolyte drinks to blood, panic, and mayhem.

Then came the fear, the shock. The rush of bomb victims poured into the tent. Blood everywhere. Bloody ears. A man came in with his ear hanging loose, blood on half of his face. A baby was in a stroller crying. Sharp sights of torn clothes and burned skin. The place of recovery became a battlefield hospital with no warning or time to think.

I froze, forgot I even had legs that could move, muscles that had just carried me through a marathon. I offered to help give blood, not thinking where my own family was.

Shock like that day strips you down to instinct and erases everything else.

The medical tent personnel told me to leave. I quickly ran to the bus. The people looked terrified, still helping runners despite it all. I grabbed my bag with a phone, remembering one awful thought. Grace. She was at the finish line. I had seen Paul and the rest of the family at BC an hour earlier.

Grace—she was just twelve years old, sixth grade—walking out of Sugar Heaven, the candy shop right next to Marathon Sports at the finish line two minutes before the bomb went off. She had paid for the candy she knew I loved to say, "Good job, Mama. I was thinking of you." She walked out of the store one hundred and twenty seconds before the bomb exploded.

Don't ever again walk through life too smug or too sure—because everything you love can be taken in two damn minutes.

You don't forget a detail like that. You don't unfeel it. And you never again take any moment for granted. She still has the tape footage from the store of her and her friend at the cashier, walking out, up the street, and boom. . .

The magic came far later. In Boston, it rewired us as a collective whole to then live differently, to support one another. I wish I could erase what I saw as I walked to the doorway of that tent away: thick smoke, ambulances, a sheer war zone, right here at that legendary finish line where people have to qualify just to get a bib number. They come from all over this world just to run through that finish line and savor that experience. The knowing still stings, but it also fills me with awe. That moment could have ended us. But it didn't. It changed us.

Boston people are just cool people; they are straightforward. That entire week felt like a movie, a manhunt, lockdown.

Boylston Street, the noisy, sweaty, wild end-of-the-marathon street, was now wrapped in yellow tape. The place where thousands of fans and feet had crossed, screaming, crying, laughing, was now sealed. Frozen in time. Evidence markers were on the sidewalk where blood had been. Storefront windows had shattered and glass was all out in front of the store my daughter had just walked out of.

The National Guard was standing with rifles, still as stone. No cheers, no cowbells. No "You got this!" Just silence, gunmetal, and sirens far away. You'd see runners—the real Boston runners—wandering near the edge of the tape. Most did not get to finish that day. They got stopped on the course; medals were mailed to them.

Race jackets on. 2013 blue and yellow. They didn't talk. They stood there like ghosts, like they'd left a part of themselves at that finish line and weren't sure if they were allowed to take it back. I remember the smell too. Not sweat. Not street food. Bleach. Metal. Burned plastic. Fear. Real, living fear.

That city spent a whole week holding its breath. Waiting for the next boom.

Waiting for the suspects. People stayed home; school was closed. The runners who had trained for months suddenly didn't care about their finish time anymore. They cared about friends, strangers, faces on the news.

Boston turned into something it had never been, a crime scene, yet underneath all that quiet, Boston's heart still beat hard. A week later, when they caught the second bomber in a backyard boat, Boston breathed again.

The stories were gut-wrenching. But the resilience was electric.

The magic came from not survival but from what it rewired. From the inside out. Everyone in Boston—every local, every runner, every cop, every bystander—got carved a little that day.

Here's the thing about Beantown: Boston people don't quit. We're built differently. Straight shooters with big hearts. Tough shells and soft centers. We show up. We don't back down.

Fear turned to ferocity. Strangers became brothers and sisters overnight. Boston didn't just recover; it transformed. It showed up in every color.

That following year, a large group of us ladies rallied around the Stepping Strong Organization, supporting a special friend who spear-headed it.

The Stepping Strong Center for Trauma Innovation was born out of the Boston Marathon bombings. It's an incredible organization dedicated to transforming trauma care for civilians and military alike. It's about more than just surviving injury; it's about rebuilding, innovating, and giving trauma victims a real chance to thrive again. What started as a response to senseless violence has become a symbol of strength, healing, and forward motion, true Boston grit at its finest.

While doing a twenty-miler in that training season one cold snowy winter day, my wise girlfriend named Karen looked me straight in the eye as I was rushing to finish. She said: "Girlfriend, what the hell are you doing? You're a damn good runner, and speed is not your issue. Just get organized, slow down, and run the slow twenties each week. Run slower with intention. Your time has just begun."

That hit me. I was usually pressed for time every day, never mindfully planning on how to best train, and it took a wise friend to tell the truth. She knew there was no dignity in letting me off the hook. It just takes one person with sincere intentions to help you see the things you don't see in yourself.

I listened to her. I ripped that last bandage off, from comfort to pain. I got organized, took my health and nutrition patterns far more seriously, brought my whole iron level panels up, and for the first time in years, I went to real hardcore physical work.

I was in bed by nine o'clock every night and decided to join the women's team at the Boston Athletic Association, which meant making the time cuts just to get on the roster and sitting through an interview. The male coach would call last minute because he always needed a third scorer for the team. And after probably five other women said no, I said yes. I was up early on a Saturday, no excuses, running my heart out.

I even got paid. Imagine that—the same girl who once quit her high school track team, racing for the BAA at age forty-seven. My running partner jumped in beside me, and together, we worked our tails off—mile after mile, season after season.

"Become aware that there are no accidents in this intelligent universe. Realize that everything that shows up in your life has something to teach you. Appreciate everyone and everything in your life." — Wayne Dyer

10

FROM SIX-MINUTE MILES TO MOTION ON PAUSE

Paying closer attention to protein intake and regular blood panels became a game-changer. When I finally got them checked, my iron levels were almost nonexistent—thanks to years of heavy periods. Once I corrected that, what used to feel like a winded struggle to hold a seven-minute pace suddenly dropped into the sixes with the same effort.

It was like flipping a switch.

I began working my ass off. I ran 5Ks, 10Ks, half marathons, track workouts, did weights, the whole damn training buffet.

Not convenient, but I had my eye on Berlin, then Boston. I did the first cycle racing with the BAA team, and once my iron levels were up, the change with the same effort was insane. I was ready to show myself the true potential I had as a runner, and it was showing.

Park City, Utah

My husband and family had the passion for skiing. Peak mileage training for the Boston Marathon is February and March. The good old grind-it-out months all runners know for a spring race. So off we went to Park

City, Utah, for Presidents' Day weekend. While they were skiing on the first day, I laced up and hit the road for a twenty-mile training run from Park City to Salt Lake and back, breathing that high-altitude air and believing again in myself, in my body, in possibility. Don't ever take a single thing for granted.

When life's good, when you're flying, when you're shaving minutes off miles and starting to dream again, be grateful because in a single moment, a random snowboarder can remind you how fragile this whole gig is.

The work inside qualifying for running for the Boston Athletic Association team was not a cakewalk. I had to have an interview, prove time cuts for 10K to 26.2 just to be looked at. Then to be accepted on the team required commitment, participation, and work. When I met the coach, he asked me to race, wear Adidas, run hard, and score for the team. So I did. I trained and ran with a fire I hadn't felt since well before the London sorrow.

That upcoming spring would be my first time racing with them for the Boston Marathon.

The following day, it was one of those perfect snowy days in Deer Valley, the fancy no-snowboarder mountain, yet the last lift tickets sold out just as I went to purchase them.

Paul and I decided to take our twins out for some ski time. After lunch, Paul grinned at me by the lift and asked, "So you want the front of the train or the caboose today?" I laughed and said, "I'll take the back. You lead."

We shuffled off the chairlift and started down our first run, me at the rear, doing the nervous mom-ski stance, glancing back and forth between the girls—and that's when I felt it.

A weight. A presence. Like a boulder barreling down behind me. Before I could turn or dodge or even yell, "Watch out!" Wham! A very large man who did not speak English slammed into me from behind, immediately taking me down hard. My body twisted sideways, skis never released, poles went flying, and I skidded fast backward down the mountain like a yard-sale ragdoll, flipping as I slid backward, seeing skiers all coming toward me. A large group of men made a shield around me like a fort to assure no more faulty hits.

I was in a shitload of immediate pain, and my knee felt like it was on fire, but I was thankful for a helmet and that I had no concussion, broken back, or neck. Paul never saw it and skied to the bottom with the girls. About thirty minutes went by. Rye guy, our son, had hiked halfway up with his ski boots on, knowing something bad must have happened.

He knew I was usually glued to the girls. The next thing I knew, I was in the red sled ambulance heading down to the emergency care.

I didn't think it was possible. Not after all I'd worked for, not now.

ACL/MCL SURGERY

The noise didn't matter; I didn't even hear it. They could not diagnose me at Park City. There was no swelling, so I crutched around all week, not wanting to drag the energy of the trip down.

But the minute I landed in Boston, I walked straight off the plane and right into the ER at Mass General. One look and they knew—the ACL/MCL was completely gone.

Stiff upper lip time. This was just another lesson in the chapter of appreciation for health, for life, but it was not the end of the book.

A friend, also one of Boston's top surgeons, was truly amazing. He took one look at my knee and said,

"You've got low swelling, strong range of motion, a good sign."

I asked him, "Can we get this done?"

He nodded. "Yes. Let's get you in fast." He scheduled the surgery for the following week. I was so deeply grateful that he knew me and was a talented, gifted surgeon. He gave me a new ACL, repaired my MCL, told me I had the smallest anatomy to work with but good cartilage, and gave me a pat on the back.

I'll never really understand why people rush straight to the negative. It's like they can't help themselves. The first thing out of their mouth is everything you can't do. They don't even realize they're doing it.

"Oh, that stinks." "You shouldn't have done that." "You'll never get back to running." "I'm sorry, Kate. Hang up your sneaks."

It's like they hand you a bag of fear before you even get a chance to try.

People love to catastrophize. Accidents and misfortune get more attention than glory.

They'll tell you what you're too fat for, what you're too skinny for. What's too risky. That you're too old. Or that it's too hard. Not me. I'm an encourager, a believer that everything is possible within reason.

I have no room for small, limited thinking.

When I came out of surgery, still groggy, braced, and iced, I found out that Will was accepted to the Noble and Greenough School for seventh grade. Paul held onto the sheet of paper they handed me like it was a life map. It broke down my healing plan: step-by-step, day-by-day. I loved that sheet. It gave me structure, clarity, and a goal. No time for pity. No time to spiral. I went straight into physical therapy.

- Swimming daily laps with a buoy between my legs
- Quad sets until they burned
- Ice
- Rest
- Repeat

This was my new training. This was the race I had to win before the next one. The physical comeback of a woman over forty-five was not something I saw coming. It was blind faith fighting against the aging wall, which slows recovery and reduces ability to build muscle.

If you had told me—right there in the middle of that nine-month ACL/MCL nightmare—that I'd heal stronger and soon run a 3:08 marathon, I would've laughed out loud. Because in that season, I was wearing a thick, clunky knee brace, slipping on ice with crutches, and wrangling toddlers into car seats in the minivan with one good leg. My only priority was being a mom—a good one.

My older two were growing up fast, grinning wide, and getting recruited for college sports. They were captains of their high school teams. And me? I was just quietly wondering if I'd ever really run again —or even walk properly—without a limp.

The mind can really spiral in recovery. The game-ready ice machine sat there, but just limping over to pick it up felt like a workout. And then the thoughts would creep in—what if my knee doesn't track right? What if, after all this damn work, I fall and make it worse?

And once again, *The Power of Now* showed up in my life—a quiet reminder to stay right here, in this moment, and just do the next small thing.

At first, I thought our dog, Jackson, was just mimicking me—moving a little slower, acting a little tired. But it turned out he had acute heart disease. He was only nine years old, and we had to put him down. Just like that. On top of everything else, I had to pick up all the kids, and we had to say goodbye to him right then and there. No warning. No time to prepare. Just one more heartbreak in a season already stacked with them.

I held on to a deeper faith in the unknown. I knew how to do that now, never taking an ounce of internal mental strength gained for granted. This was bad timing; it was nothing, and accidents happen.

Then came an angel. A sweet, cool man named Alex Petruska—my PT man at Mass General. He was a miracle worker, a straight shooter. The guy took one look at me, sized me up as a late-forties cupcake looking to get back to yoga maybe. Then I revealed who I was and what I intended to do. So he invested in me and knew I wasn't screwing around. I got my fire back. "No time to waste, Alex. Let's go, man. We're doing this, Alex, you and me." Quad sets, glute bridges, clamshells, and comparison of strength from left to right—he pushed me, and I loved it.

Strength, structure, repetition, and above all—consistency. I gave my body what it needed: ice, great food, rest, and I told it what I expected. It didn't happen overnight; it was not easy. But day after day, inch by inch—my body responded. That's what I learned. The body listens when you love it the right way.

The feeling of falling, slipping, going backward when I had babies, teens, toddlers, and a full house of mischief was real. Yet the faith I gained in believing in the dream kept me going.

The giddyap. The fire in my belly. The little whisper every day said, *Keep going. You've got something waiting for you on the other side of this.* And here's the kicker: that something? It was a series of faster times I never knew I could complete, not at my age. 3:10s, 3:14s, then a 3:08 marathon at age forty-nine.

Not despite the injury but because of it. Because injury forces you to slow down, tune in, and rebuild from the foundation. And that foundation was built from the dark cave.

11

BOSTON IN MY BONES

Boston Strong. I had never been prouder to call a place home.

In 2017, my running buddy and I had momentum, and it was building. We could both feel it. And in classic Boston fashion, a Nor'easter rolled in for the first marathon we ran together with the BAA and Stepping Strong. Temps hovered at thirty-seven, near record lows. This was nothing for her. Relentless rain, twenty-five to thirty-five-mile-per-hour headwinds, gusts over forty-five-miles-per-hour blasting in our faces, and more than two inches of cold rain fell that year. She thought nothing of the heavy downpours and puddles, which drenched us from start to finish.

I, on the other hand, was immediately treated for hypothermia. She was just fine. Many dropped out midrace, including top contenders. We both finished somewhere around 3:20 for 26.2. I had soaked bloody shoes, one rain glove on, one left on the course, and hands too cold to take the other one off.

April 15, 2019

Grace, now a senior in high school, was accepted at Middlebury College, training for her first marathon, and raising funds for Brigham and

Women's Stepping Strong Organization. It was race day. The temps crept up toward seventy degrees, which for Boston feels like summer in April.

My running pal and I had put in a solid season of training and half-joked during long runs, "Oh my God, could you imagine if we actually win the female masters?" We were laughing at ourselves. Like, who says that? But then—we actually did it! Three scorers, a sub-3:10, 3:14, 3:24. Magic. By one minute.

My daughter finished just behind us. Talk about a full-circle moment. A mother, her run partner, and her kid, all crossing the same finish line, miles and years apart. It was something I'll never forget.

The BAA held a beautiful award ceremony at the Copley Plaza Hotel. My girl got us matching jackets, which tied a beautiful bow around the occasion.

Joan Benoit, the famous Olympian runner, was now talking to us about the NESCAC schools.

Check the life dream box! We stood on stage with Joan Benoit Samuelson.

The best part is we truly did not ever think it would happen. Another example: If you just show up, you never know. Seeing Grace brought me right back to that moment, to those two minutes that changed everything. Two minutes between safety and fear. Between what was and what would never be the same again. It's wild how time unfolds like that. One glance at her, strong and grown, and suddenly, I was standing at that finish line all over again, another reminder to never take what is precious for granted.

Stepping Strong Ladies, the tribe who believed, cared for me—when I didn't even believe in myself. Boston had bled. Boston had mourned, but now it was Boston Strong once again.

Resilience isn't just a word; it's a way of life. It does not have to come in run fashion. It comes after the period of any kind of pain, the resurrection of anyone's human spirit in real life, and in real relationships. It is in the real that everything changes.

I had previously been, by far, the slowest runner in our little crew. Dead last on every group run. The caboose. The "Wait, where's Kate?" I preferred it that way. I liked being in the back, the place with no expectations, just humor.

Until the day I decided I didn't. Something stronger shifted inside, not out of ego but of gut instinct. I was ready to give more.

This shift was a powerful turning point for me in my life. Taking full ownership, not just of what is possible or convenient but also of the things that are easy to ignore, blow off, and even easier to make excuses for. Accountability is power.

The kind of pivot doesn't come with fireworks but with a fierce little whisper from a gal who had pain in her life that says: Let's go. After chaos, grief, and survival, this is where you start to reclaim your strength, not just to endure but to rise with purpose doing it your own way.

After a major injury, the world slows down, and it can be beneficial to teach yourself some new tricks.

At first, I resisted. Thought it was time to maybe learn the piano, maybe do some chair fitness. I started noticing things I'd never seen before, like the deeper aspect of our incredible, amazing human body's ability to heal and work back from acute injury, of our fascia, tendons, and range of mobility.

It was the first time I slowed way down and noticed that one side of my body was far stronger than the other. One was carrying all the weight. The other side? Weak, atrophied, quiet. My glute strength, foot control, IT band—all lopsided. Muscles I'd never even thought about before were suddenly speaking up, showing me just how much I'd been ignoring them. Turns out, all strength isn't always balanced, and the body keeps the score. Half the time, we don't think of it.

Coordination, form, foot strike, flexibility, and mind became more responsive and in tune because the injured knee had atrophied. It felt foreign to me—thin, unreliable, weak. Yet slowly, through movement, grace, and work, it started to come back. So did I.

I didn't realize it at the time, but the words from *The Power of Now* by Eckhart Tolle settled somewhere deeper inside me. So when the grief gutted my life, they rose up.

It helped my racing and my relationships for sure. I tuned in, not out. This is proof for us all to tune in deeper and find your best result. Tune out and you won't.

The only downside to tuning in and not tuning out—my personal practice of *The Power of Now*—was that I was late to pretty much everything. Disorganized half the time. Never knew where my keys were. Ever. But you know what? I was fiercely present—in mind, body, and heart.

And that's a rare and liberating thing as a mother and a friend. I never cared to judge, criticize, or comment because my kids felt me there. Fully. Even if the backpack, diaper bag was forgotten and the coffee was cold, I was all in.

"In the depth of winter, I finally learned that there was in me an invincible summer." —Albert Camus

12

THE BEAUTIFUL RIPPLE EFFECTS OF GRIEF

Rebelling against your handicaps gets you nowhere. Neither does self-pity. My real adventure is to accept every possibility —and play the most interesting game in the world: making the best of it.

That was my full circle moment.

2023 World Marathon Majors Championships, London, a decade later, is different. The long game—the real dream—was always to make it back to where it all began, London. The city where my love for running first woke up. And not just to run London again but to earn that World Marathon Majors bib. To come full circle.

And when it finally happened, it was more beautiful than I ever imagined. There I was, standing at the start line—not the crowded, noisy start from years past—but our own private entrance. VIP every-thing. Fancy porta-potties that didn't smell like defeat. A separate start line away from the chaos, quiet and calm like a breath held just before dawn.

On my bib were the footprints and handprints of Sam and Myles. My boys. Carried with me every step of the way. Their marks pressed into my heart and now onto that race, as if they were running right alongside me.

It wasn't just a race—it was the closing of a circle. A return to the beginning, only this time stronger, braver, and more whole. Each finish line wasn't an end—it was a becoming. Each mile was a meditation in gratitude. I wasn't running to get away from life—but deeper into it.

The Power of True Kindness

The favorite, most intense moments of our lives really start here.

I remember lying in the hospital bed, my good friend sitting next to me. She showed up on that dark day, the gross feeling of a hospital room in London. She took the shift to just sit next to me. She just sat there with me, feeling that same empty awfulness. Her beautiful lipstick was on and nails were done in stunning contrast to me. She was not family, yet she cared like family. But as she sat there, she said, "I want to do something different in my life, with purpose going forward."

She valued and added to that moment so deeply. Emotionally, that is really hard to do with and for someone you're not related to. In a terrible moment, most people don't show up. She did. That is the definition of a friend. Kindness isn't loud. It's not always headline-worthy or Instagrammable. It's not measured in medals or split times or square footage. It lives in the subtleties—the tiny, blink-and-you-miss-it moments that actually make a life.

It's in the neighbor whose driver picks you up when you can't walk. It is being there and in it without saying a word. The friend who shows up with coffee just when you didn't know you needed it. The stranger who frames your brother's quote from high school after he dies, drops it off, and holds the door, and makes eye contact, like they see you. It is in the realtor who seemed to understand you need a home and lands it for you.

It's not performative—it's presence. For a long time, I thought I had to keep performing. Run faster, juggle more, sell more, make better paychecks, keep the house standing, the kids alive, the marriage hot and steady, and the laundry mountain from swallowing us whole. Eventually, I realized—it's really not about doing any of it at all.

It's just about how you truthfully, authentically present yourself, how you show up. With your cup full, your eyes bright, and ears ready to listen with your time. With your heart in your hands. I've never been a great planner. I won't win awards for organization. But kindness? That I can do. That's where my feet always land when everything else feels like too much: Be kind. Show up. Slow down. Look someone in the eye and see them. It's not about status. It's not about having the perfect life. It's about being a soft place for someone else to land. Let that be enough because it truly is.

When I was with and played with my kids, I was with them—fully. When I made sandwiches, I noticed their little hands, their smirks, the way they licked the knife when they thought I wasn't looking. The back talk, the whining, the mischief. I wore their souls around me like armor. Their fears. Their quirks. Their quiet talents. Their everything.

I didn't just know my kids—I absorbed them.

Find Your Magic

I've become extremely resilient, emotionally, mentally, and physically, not because I placed on podiums and ran fast marathons, but because I tuned out the noise.

The real magic became showing up at school drop-off with hair still wet from a run, sneakers crusted with dirt from the trail, kids laughing (or crying) in the backseat, and somehow holding it all together with nothing but coffee, stubbornness, and a little quiet magic that comes from knowing you've done something hard before 7 a.m.

The magic comes from knowing who you are fully and how you can best serve, teach, and show up for others.

Magic is laughing when you're wiping peanut butter off the wall, signing a school permission slip, and answering a work call calmly and smoothly while someone is knocking on the door.

Magic is in that peace of trusting the road and loving the chaos.

When the husband's gone, the dog has shit all over the house, the kids are hungry, the kitchen is a mess, and when they all need you all at once, the magic is in just being calm, present, and fully "there." Enjoying and appreciating the moment and ignoring the rest.

When you've touched really hard stuff, whatever that may be

emotionally, and you've chosen life again, you will love in layers that other people don't see or feel or understand on the same level.

You don't love your life, kids, husband, and friends from the surface. You love them so deeply from the bottom of the ocean that the waves don't matter. And that decade of sheer and utter presence all came from that dark cave years prior.

Sure, exercise and running helped. Yes, it gave me discipline, structure, and oxygen when life felt too tight. But the real fuel behind the races, the resilience, and the recovery was the meaningful time with certain friendships.

It was joy and purpose, not in perfection but in presence. When you love like that and do it with your whole, broken, beating heart, it will always love you back. The magic finds you and fills you. I promise it does.

13

FACE YOUR FEARS EVEN WHEN YOU'RE CLUELESS AND SCARED SHITLESS

Discipline doesn't look heroic, but it is what builds the life you quietly crave.

If I was going to pivot, take a break from running, save my knees, and try a different race, I wasn't showing up for a participation ribbon. Nope. No time to waste. I wanted a medal.

Problem was—I had absolutely no real background in two-thirds of this triathlon game. If you break it down:

- Fear of speed and falling
- Fear of drowning and open water
- Fear of claustrophobia

I don't trust anything that straps my feet into a machine going twenty miles per hour with hairpin turns and wind gusts that could knock me off a bike. So naturally, I signed up for the Nantucket triathlon. The swim? Pure panic. That's not a "Zen" experience—it's a mosh pit in water. No lanes. No walls to push off. Just bodies, feet in your face, elbows flailing, and a deep "What the hell am I doing here?" moment right before the horn blows. The bike? Feels like riding a missile with no brakes and a helmet flying off the head.

You're locked into your pedals, hunched over, praying you don't fall, praying the wind doesn't take you out, praying you don't miss the turn and end up in the woods. Yet here's what I learned about fear: You don't beat it by pretending it's not there. You beat it by outsmarting it. So the night before the race? I got in my car right before dark and drove the entire course. I imagined myself on the bike, even trying to lean while driving like I was on the bike.

Corner by corner. Turn by turn. I felt the handlebars in my hands, even though I had only ridden the bike once. I saw the course unfold like a movie in my head and, no, it wasn't brave. It was just strategic. Because I'm not tough; I'm just a pansy with a plan. Fake it till you make it? Damn right. Winging it like a free bird, and it is working. Same goes for the water.

I practiced in the pool, sure—but mostly, I practiced not panicking. I learned how to sight and how to breathe and how to be okay with chaos because the chaos in all race formats isn't going away, but your reaction to it can change everything.

I didn't have time to be perfect, but I did have time to be intentional. I didn't have years of bike or swim practice, but I had a race, a goal, and a good bike; that was enough. I sure as hell wasn't coming home empty-handed after going all the way to Nantucket with a bike.

Gun goes off. The bravery of the beginner. I wasn't trying to be fast —I was trying not to die in the swim. Here it comes, heart-racing fear. So I let everyone go, so the water was calm when I got in, and I had space. I went on my back and finished last, dead last. I didn't quite understand the transition. That was a race, too, so I skipped socks and winged it, helmet practically flying off the back of my head, breathing through my nose like a monk on a mountain, praying Hail Marys under my breath, knowing one crack in road, strange turn, or biker too close could result in a fall, wipe my knee reconstruction, and more.

The biker ladies were not my type, at least not that day. There was a woman—big, solid, fearless. Real biker lady, gloves and all, she'd cruise past me downhill like a bullet.

Then when the uphills came, me being lightweight, I would naturally pass her, not because I was trying to, but because the gravity made it. So back and forth, back and forth, I was literally praying, pedaling, saying Hail Marys, and taking deep breaths while she kept pulling up next to me, eyes lit, and said, "Hey, you wanna play this game? Let's go! Come on!"

Oh no. Lady, I'm just trying to stay upright, eyes glued five feet ahead, and not take anybody out with me. I looked at her and said, "I'm so sorry, lady. I don't even know what you're talking about." She was not very kind. The run community, they pat you on the back when they pass you. I do. I made it to the end of the bike course, even when I had to physically stop, clip out to make certain turns. Then I got sneaks on, and I cranked it, 6:40 pace. When I was just about to finish, I ran by the mean biker lady, patted her on the back, and gave her a thumbs-up. Then, I got to stand on the podium. It was ninety degrees, too. Feel the fear and do it anyway.

A trick I wish someone had told me before I started pretending to be a triathlete: If you're gonna stick your face in the ocean and swim like you mean it, you better learn how to breathe. Simple, right? Not really. Ocean water is cold. People are everywhere. Your adrenaline is spiking, and your brain is screaming, "You're gonna drown, idiot!" But here's the secret: Blow. Bubbles. Yep. That's it. Before the horn even sounds, put your face in the water and blow bubbles like a five-year-old in a bathtub. Why? Because your body starts to realize: I'm safe. I can breathe, and it resets the panic. It gets your rhythm started before chaos hits. Now, if that fails? No problem. Flip over. Float on your back. Regroup. Start again. No shame. No drama. This ain't the Olympics. It's just a bunch of grown-ups in spandex.

I didn't look like I belonged out there, not even as a runner, I didn't. Everyone around me looked like sleek, tanned dolphins—gliding through the water like it was second nature. Me? I was a panicked fish in Target fog-filled goggles with a stubborn Irish heart and a refusal to quit. So flip on the back, look at the clouds, and kick! Forget trying to breathe, sight, swallow water perfectly.

So, here's your invitation: Pick something that scares you. Something really hard. Something you've been avoiding because it's uncomfortable and you're not sure you'll be good at it. And do it. On purpose. Not because you're fearless but because you're not—and that's exactly what makes it powerful.

14

UPROOTED: A NEW START LINE

I care far more about the home, the feel, the soul of the place, while Paul barely seems to notice, as long as there's Wi-Fi and a working fridge.

Maybe it's because for women, especially mothers, the home is the stage where everything happens. It's not just walls and a roof. It's the place where the backpacks drop, where the meals are made, where the laundry piles and the memories stack. It's where birthdays get decorated for, and homework gets argued over. It's where you know the morning light in the kitchen or how the floor creaks near the kitchen window. Owning a home means roots. Control. A little piece of this wild life that you actually own—not something borrowed, not something temporary. It matters. It feels permanent in a world that rarely is.

But men? As long as the shower works and the remote's close by, they're fine. Renting, owning, apartment, house—what's the difference?

Because they don't build the life inside those walls the way we do. We see the house as an extension of the family. And they—well—they just see a place that holds the people they love.

And maybe that's okay. Because someone's got to care about the curtains. And someone's got to pretend they do. Balance, right?

When Paul gave his twenty-year speech for Capital Group in camera lights at our home in Boston during COVID, he was emotional. He had been working L.A. hours from Boston, late calls bleeding into after dinner, chasing something three time zones away. And after twenty years in the same career, everything was shifting. Changing. And the truth was hard to ignore, even if I wanted to: the writing was on the wall.

If he wanted to stay in the game, which we needed to, we'd have to all go. He had been told to go to L.A. right after London, yet I held him back.

I felt it, dragging behind every conversation, every plan. Los Angeles called for years; it was impossible to fight, and I was never close to ready.

A few close friends reminded me by saying, at this stage, "Kate? Wow? That's a tall order for you at this stage of life."

See, my husband, he's built far more like water. He bends with the wind. He can switch time zones, beds, cars, careers, like he is changing socks. Drop him in a new system and he swims through the bigger waves one at a time, calmly, slowly. Adaptation is really nothing for him.

Me? My dad is still in the home I grew up in. I need structure, people, and places I can count on, familiarity. If not same-same, I can lose a tad bit of brain functionality.

Not just walls and a roof but in consistency of habits. It is comforting to live in a place where you know the feeling of the character of the ones who live around you.

A place where you know which drawer holds the supplements, pens, tape, and where the extras are. Where you can find the scissors, sport shirt, and towel when the kids need them five minutes before school.

Raising a family isn't just dinner and driving. It's holding up the entire damn blueprint of a family infrastructure in your head as well as extended family and friends within a large community while focusing on growth, paying attention to teachers, schools, report cards, progress, the passwords, permission slips, the doctor, orthodontist appointments, lost library books, birthdays, coaches' names, celebrations, and the school secretary's name and face. It's remembering who likes who, who needs what, forward planning, and medical needs.

It organizes schedules, tournament travel, teacher gifts, Halloween costumes, get-togethers on weekends, birthdays, Thanksgiving, Christmas, Easter, Fourth of July, and graduations.

Home is the only backdrop that makes that work. The grill, garden, and pantry you know by heart. The bathroom cabinet that holds every cough drop, Band-Aid, and thermometer in its exact spot. The safe zone, quiet spots where you regroup, sit with your coffee, and take a breath.

When you move, no matter how prepared or organized, you lose all that. The roots rip up. The muscle memory of home is gone, and suddenly, you're forgetting passwords, missing emails, and double-booking sports practices because nothing feels familiar. You can't find the tape. You can't find yourself.

For me, home is not shelter; it's my full mental map. The one that holds the family together. Losing that map feels like dropping all the balls at once. It's disorienting, exhausting, and no one really talks about how hard that really is. Willie was a great teacher. He was such a champ. The girls, too, Paul, the same.

Ouch, but me? I needed a time-out, like a toddler. I underestimated the confusion in a culture change on top of having three kids to adapt.

This hit like a bitch slap.

Three kids, new schools, a brand-new city sprawling out in every direction, and me dead last on the list. L.A. felt like stepping into a movie scene I didn't audition for, where nobody warned me that the script was real life.

Will, starting fresh as a junior at Loyola High School, took the wheel and celebrated every minute.

When you've grown up in Boston, real Boston, not the postcard version with the swan boats and cobblestone romance, but the Dunkin' in your veins, side-eye-at-strangers kind of Boston, yes, you think you've got the world figured out. Order. Control. Predictability.

You know where to park without getting towed. You know which guy to call when a rat winds up in your townhome. You know that "How are ya?" doesn't mean "Tell me your feelings." It means "keep movin', kid." It's a city that teaches you survival by elbows and sarcasm. Like Wahlberg with a chipped tooth, grinning because he knows the rules and you don't.

So you pack up that suitcase—full of confidence, old boots, maybe some Harvard fleeces or an East Coast sweatshirt if you're feeling fancy —and you think, "L.A.? No big deal. Sunshine's just Boston without the snow. I got this."

But L.A. doesn't care what you think you've got. They don't care about your education, your cute family, your roots. The strangers smile on purpose and don't really "care."

So there you are . . . fresh off the plane from Boston, survival skills and lingo packed tight. Quick comebacks. Sharp edges. Sarcasm locked and loaded. Like you're ready for a snowstorm in February.

Except . . . you've just landed in L.A. And L.A. is not February.

It's sunshine, surfboards, screenplays. Everyone's in "the business." The barista? Writing a pilot. Your neighbor? Starring in a yogurt commercial. The dog walker? Voiceover work on the side.

Meanwhile, I'm standing there holding my East Coast attitude like a snow shovel at a Malibu beach party. Totally the wrong tool for the job. "Wait, you don't have a screenplay?" someone actually asked me. "Nope," I said. "But I've got some kickass sneakers, a mean casserole, and a Costco card."

Silence. Crickets. Probably because that doesn't get you a callback in L.A.

In Boston, confidence keeps you alive. In L.A., confidence makes you weird. Out here, they don't bark. They float. And that's the thing no one tells you when you move your life 3,000 miles west thinking you've got all the right tools in your emotional suitcase: you don't. You left half of what you need behind. And the other half? It's totally outdated. How's that for confidence?

It's disorienting. It's lonely. And maybe another life lesson, where the real starting line is.

I was thrown into it all like a menopausal granny in slow motion, gripping the wheel while Teslas zipped past and horns blared like some city-wide alarm clock.

Paul would say, "Yeah, Kate. Why don't you just go play some golf or maybe go for a run!"

I was wandering the streets of Santa Monica in my running gear, looking totally lost, dead phone in hand like it was a useless brick. No

GPS, no clue. I swear, I got clipped by the same homeless guy on a bike at least twice—maybe three times. Tents lined the beach like a weird campground gone sideways. I was ducking, dodging, weaving my way down the California incline like I was in some kind of urban obstacle course, muttering, "What is this place?" under my breath.

Meanwhile, Paul was sitting in his nice, clean, stellar office, totally unaware that his wife was out there trying not to get run over.

We take for granted the little systems that hold our lives together— the familiar faces, knowing which doctor to call, where the kids' appointments are, the clubs, the schools, the places that become our second home.

In L.A., I felt like I was constantly behind, struggling just to catch up with the pace of it all. Like everyone else had the map, and I was still trying to figure out which way was north.

I was in a land of Botox and twenty-five-year-olds as "life coaches." I was in a totally different culture, plain and simple, stepping onto a movie set where the script forgot to warn me this was real life. One part sunshine and palm trees. One part lock your doors and keep your head down. Did I make a good first impression here? Oh, God, help me, I absolutely did not.

To be fair, since landing in California, we have lived in fifteen different homes across three towns, which is probably why I still laugh every time I tap "home" in the GPS because honestly . . . which one?

But if there was a Most Improved Award for adaptation and attitude adjustment, I'd win it hands down.

I've learned more about self-joy in flexibility and patience in starting over than I ever signed up for.

Turns out, home isn't just a place; it's a moving beautiful target you just carry with you.

Making true, real friends for life? Midlife? Who the hell has the mental and emotional energy for that with an established busy family? Nobody can replicate twenty-, thirty-, or fifty-year-old friendships and community overnight, but you can show up and start again.

Sometimes, grit doesn't come screaming down the hallway. Sometimes, it tiptoes in with a golf bag slung over one shoulder and a quiet determination in its eyes. It looks like stepping onto a skateboard or the edge of the deep end, where falling and drowning feel like real possibilities. Where your brain says stop, but your gut whispers maybe just try. And if you're lucky or maybe just brave enough, you vote yes.

Yes to the risk. Yes to the thrill. Yes to seeing how it plays out. Yes to rooting for your husband, partner, or wife. That's what no one tells you: courage isn't always loud. Sometimes, it's just showing up to the edge, toes hanging off, and saying, "Okay, let's see what happens."

Because even fear has ripple effects. But guess what? So does faith. Not to prove the world wrong but to remind yourself you're still in the damn fight.

15

LET'S TALK ABOUT PUSHING THROUGH YOUR MILE TWENTY-THREE

The stretch in every marathon where everything you've got left is put on trial: mile twenty-three to twenty-six.

The ripple zone is the crucible. That's where the real work lives. It's physical, sure. Your legs go numb but still scream. Your breath? Shallow. Tight. The muscles you spent sixteen weeks training suddenly feel like they've been swapped with cinder blocks. Blisters? Check. Cramps? Check. The bizarre, floaty, out-of-body sensation that makes you question if your feet are even touching the ground? Absolutely. But the pain doesn't stop there. No, the real beast shows up in your brain.

Now, you're in the tunnel. Your focus narrows. You stop noticing crowds, signs, cheers, even your playlist.

It's just you, the clock, and the battlefield between your ears. You start bargaining. "I could walk the rest." "I've come far enough." "Does this even matter?" And yet, you keep going. Why? Because for sixteen weeks or more, you've been building toward this one single day. You skipped parties. You sacrificed sleep. You did life and worked hard to train alongside it.

You shut down the voice that said, "Not today," and laced up anyway. You followed a plan. You trained in the rain, the dark, the early morning cold. You counted your miles, hoping they'd be enough, and when race day comes, there are no guarantees. The basics you did daily should beat brilliance, right?

Your body might betray you. Your stomach might flip. Your hormones might go rogue. The weather could also throw a tantrum, especially in Boston. You might do everything precisely right—and there's still a big chance to fall apart.

So, what do you do? You have to let it go. You surrender all control without surrendering effort.

You accept that this last brutal stretch is the price of showing up for something bigger than comfort.

The only ripple effect I can honestly speak to: that finish line feeling doesn't stop at the line. It becomes part of your DNA. It shows up when life blindsides you. When grief hits. When your life plans fall apart. When someone dies. When money matters and there isn't enough. When chaos and trauma feel too heavy.

When life falls apart, no one's clapping, nothing makes any sense at all, and you can't see the finish line.

It shows up when you walk forward anyway, when your kids watch you get back up. It shows up in your posture and the way you breathe through pain. It shows up in the way there's no hiding from it.

It's the reminder that you are made of something that doesn't quit —even when everything and everyone else does.

That's the day you know you're the one who rewrites your story.

Every single year on April 15, when I hit mile twenty-three in Brookline where my mom grew up, it brings me right back to the black hole, the cave, the hospital room in London when I woke up wanting to be in heaven. That mile twenty-three is my checkpoint, a reminder to myself of how damn lucky I am.

Mile Twenty-Three: When Body & Mind Break

Quads, hamstrings, calves, feet, toes—all throbbing. Joints stiff, IT band screaming. The pavement's pounding takes its toll. Every breath of air you take feels thin, like you're sucking for air that won't come. Muscles cramp, ribs spasm, twitching without warning—ready to seize. Blisters form and bleed; skin shaves raw. You feel totally shredded. It's where your real race starts.

You try to dig. Push past the fear. Past the quitting voice and find something deeper. Resolve. Or you don't make it.

It doesn't matter if your goal is a 6:30-minute mile or a 10:30-minute mile, the exuded effort, based on time for each runner, feels the exact same.

The finish line feels close—and impossibly far. One more step seems unbearable. It's very simple: it's all between the ears now. Will you hold pace? Will you push? Or will you break? You feel on the edge of despair. A sheer intensity of effort and vulnerability.

This is when the work you put into yourself shows up, the internal dialogue: You, my friend, you just hold on now, just hold on, and you'll be right there before you know it.

Many runners describe a beauty in that pain—a kind of transcendence because it strips everything else away, highlighting all that's left—you and your raw will.

For about ten years, my oldest son—especially in his teenage prime—really leaned into being the alpha dog. And to be fair, he earned it. He was a great kid. Sharp. Competitive. Excellent squash player, solid golfer, good student. Confident as hell. And me? I was just "Mom." He loved to rib me, to tell me I wasn't really athletic.

I'd roll my eyes, maybe toss a sock at him, but I never really had the energy to fight back. Still, I'd climb into bed most nights with a little smug smile on my face—because while the boys were busy debating definitions, I was out there actually doing it. Bleeding through marathons, pushing strollers up hills, dodging emotional landmines with toddlers strapped to my chest. Not athletic? Please. I was training for the Olympics of life.

What I should've said was: "All right, boys—until you've been diligently committed to running fifty to seventy miles a week, year after year, for a solid decade, then you can tell me how unathletic I am.

But until then? Keep swinging your golf clubs and sinking your putts.

Mile twenty-three is what we all search for.

That dark hallway between who you were and who you're about to become.

It's when the mind decides how to suffer. It's when you stop resisting and start receiving. Receiving the pain in the moment, the miracle of simply breathing and being alive.

It's not the glorious starting line, full of promise and fresh legs. It's not the finish, where medals and cameras and relief wait.

So maybe you're not a runner, nor do you even care about mile two or twenty-three.

Maybe you're in a tricky relationship that you want to quit.

Maybe you're grinding in a job and getting nowhere. Maybe you're terminally sick and are giving up.

Mile twenty-three is in you, too, I promise you. Think of the place where your body and mind are begging to stop. Where the easy option, the quiet quitting, the safe turning back—start whispering in your ear. The place where you wonder why you ever signed up for it in the first place.

The place where you can discover yourself past your own circumstances. In your life when the moment comes to make the decision you don't want to make.

Leave the job that pays the bills but kills the soul. End that relationship that drains you but feels safe and familiar. Move forward into a place where the ground feels shaky and every voice inside you says, "Stay. It's safer here. It's known here."

Mile twenty-three is where comfort dies. And with it, the old version of you does too.

Because breaking away, really breaking away, takes more than desire. It takes mental strength. The unglamorous kind. The quiet, trembling, tired kind that says: I will keep going. I will do the hard thing. And I will be OK—even when I have no proof that I will.

This is the cruel mercy of growth: No one's coming to carry you. There's no shortcut. There is no magic mile. It's just you and your willingness to lean into discomfort. To trade certainty for the terrifying promise of something better. To trust that what's on the other side of this pain is not death—but life.

I've run enough miles to know this truth: The miracle isn't mile one when everything's possible. The miracle is in mile twenty-three—when everything hurts, when you want to stop—and you choose to keep going anyway.

The idea of starting a business is the easy part; the endurance is when the business is broken, and you find a way through the storm.

That's what it takes to leave what's toxic. Hard, painful choices. To say goodbye when it breaks your heart. To decide that negative and toxic people won't rent space in your head. Mile twenty-three is when you choose to raise the rent and kick them out.

To choose the scary new beginning over and over vs. the safe, slow dying. Mile twenty-three is where the real race is run. In marathons but mainly in life.

Where the Real Work Begins

The idea part is the easy part. Take the job, start a business, stop eating sugar, quit drinking, or move your life and family across the country. Begin again. It sounds exciting. Inspiring. Like the first fresh mile of a marathon when your legs are light, and your heart is full, and you think —I've got this. But mile twenty-three is where your truth shows up.

Starting something new, like a habit, a business, a marriage, a move, a new life—that's not the hard part. That's the dream. The pitch deck. The new address written neatly in your phone. The fresh notebook. The perfect Christmas card. The untouched running shoes. Yet, at some point, comes your mile twenty-three.

The place where the glow fades and where boredom, fear, and lack of discipline creep in. Where doubt gets loud. Where you can't coach yourself. I felt it a bit right after the move to Los Angeles. What began as a brave, planned, thought-out idea turned into quiet, awkward rooms where I didn't know anyone. Streets that felt strange. Smiles that didn't speak my language. I thought I'd brought all the tools I needed in my suitcase—confidence, hustle, charm. But none of them worked here. A seasoned, experienced racer. But I was a beginner again at mile twenty-three.

And then after buying a home, renovating it, buying land, landscaping it, the fires rolled in and in a blink of an eye, the bulk of 35,000 people in this town lost their homes. Their roots. Their memories. Their sense of safety. They, too, landed at mile twenty-three—not just in their marathons but in their lives. No one plans for that mile. No one packs for it. It finds you. Ready or not.

Here's What Mile Twenty-Three Taught Me

If you build the muscle to cope with this—this broken, breathless, doubt-filled mile—you build the strength that touches every other part of your life. When you don't quit here, you won't quit there. When you lean into the pain here, you'll have grit when the relationship gets hard, when the business fails, when the next fire comes. When you finish this mile, you know you can finish any mile.

The only gift I have in my back pocket is discipline. It shows up daily, whether my emotions do or not. The ripple effect of courage is real. I promise you it is. Mile twenty-three is where that ripple starts. So start the business. Feel the pain, make the move, dream the wild dream. Take the chance. But don't lie to yourself. The hard mile is coming. And when it does, you have to be prepared to lean in. Because the magic— that strange, holy, impossible magic—only shows up for people who dare to reach past mile twenty-three and keep going. That's the real leap. That's where everything changes.

At Boston's historic post-COVID October Marathon, everything still felt strange. No crowds. No sporting events. No races for over a year. No noise. Vaccination proof and mask protocols just to pick up a bib. They cut the marathon field down to a fraction of the size. Only a quarter of runners were invited back for this—only one in one hundred twenty years of history, a unique October race. My girl and I made the cut. So despite the recent move to California, I knew I wanted to line up for it. It would be a time in history.

But life had fully slowly unraveled in a way I didn't see coming, both externally and internally. We'd moved to Los Angeles in the middle of August. Boxes were everywhere. We decided to rent our home in Boston to a famous hockey player and his family. Life's belongings went to a storage container, and the six-week house we rented sight unseen just to get our feet in the door was dark with a broken stove and quirky old electrical systems, which seemed extra confusing. It had telephone wires above a pool? It wasn't just a trip to L.A.; it was our new life. A different vibe and feel. We had neighbors close by that didn't say, "Hello," or "Welcome." High price tags on everything. Gas, food, and basics. Two girls watched their mom's every move. I was not proud of myself. I gotcha. The rental home had beds that felt like camping pads slapped onto broken frames. The bedding was thin and scratchy, like it had survived one too many Airbnb turnover days. Everything creaked, sagged, or poked. And on top of that, I was neck-deep in new routines, new learning curves, and no bathtub—just a lonely stand-up shower that judged me every time I tried to soak sore marathon legs in it.

So I figured, fine. I'll go to the beach. Saltwater heals, right? I showed up ready to recover—legs sore, soul tired—only to notice something strange: No one was in the ocean. I asked someone, "Why is the water completely empty?" They said, "Oh, stingrays. You can't go in unless you shuffle." And I'm like, "Shuffle? What do you mean—like the party shuffle? The dance floor shuffle? Or the 'get me the hell out of here' shuffle?" I was just supposed to know there were sea creatures and stealth bacteria waiting to wreck my legs worse than the marathon. Southern California wasn't just a relocation—it was an obstacle course in disguise. They toss around 'June gloom' and 'May gray' like it's some kind of secret code. I was constantly playing catch-up—new lingo, new routines, a thousand little learning curves. And nobody explained anything.

In Boston, people might be blunt, but they'll take the time to show you how things work. There's an unspoken code: If someone's lost, you help them. You educate. You care. But in L.A.? You ask a stranger something basic—like where to park or if stingrays will attack you—and they just shrug and go, "I dunno," like it's a badge of honor. Like not knowing is part of the brand. I wasn't just adjusting to a new place. I was adjusting to a whole new way of being ignored.

At the end of the day, priority one was always the kids. They needed to feel safe and happy. That was the baseline. But quietly, underneath that, I was struggling. There were days I'd be out running, legs aching, head spinning, and I'd think—if I just dropped on the trail right now, would anyone even notice? Would anyone care? Paul was too busy. He wasn't looking. I felt like I was doing all of this alone.

But it was a wake-up call, in its own way. Because it made me realize just how rare it is to feel truly supported. To have good friends, the kind who really know you, who show up without being asked. You can't re-create that overnight. Trying to drop a six-week high-volume training cycle into a brand-new life—while still acclimating, constantly on demand, emotionally off-balance—it was like trying to squeeze a marathon into a pressure cooker. And without that deep, familiar support system? It just didn't hold the same.

The roads made no sense. The manners, the entitlement? Paul was adjusting to a whole new business, trying to keep his head above water. And I was still "Mom" to my older two—who were off at college but still very much mine. So the tug-of-war between both coasts was real. And every time I had to go to the doctor, it felt like a mini adventure through madness. Sunset Boulevard would split in two—one way veered left, the other right, both full of potholes and chaos. I'd be dodging traffic cones, watching for motorcycles, blowing out two tires like it was just part of the deal. It wasn't just getting from point A to point B. It was navigating a whole new life with no map and a car that might fall apart under me.

And then—somewhere around mile eight of running completely in the wrong direction, up and down unfamiliar hills, phone dead, sweat stinging my eyes—I found myself thinking about my mother.

She never drove on the highway. Her arthritic hands made her nervous behind the wheel. But one day, she had to drive all six of us up to Essex Country Club because my dad was getting some award. No GPS back then—just paper directions and prayer.

I watched her get completely flustered. She pulled the car over, slammed her hands on the steering wheel, lit up a Virginia Slim, banged her hands again, and shouted, "Jesus, Mary, and God's name—where the hell are we?"

And there I was decades later, running wild through unfamiliar streets, feeling just as lost. Only difference was, I didn't have a cigarette —just sore legs, a dying phone, and a mother's echo in my head. I learned real quick: Don't ask a stranger for directions in California. Bad idea. People out here are completely comfortable saying "I don't know."

And not in an apologetic way—it's more like they enjoy not knowing. Like it's part of the vibe. Nobody seems to know where the hell they are, and somehow, they're fine with that.

God, I missed my running partner. She was sensible. Organized. Strategic. She could troubleshoot a GPS fail like a pro and had the kind of strong, steady head you needed when confusion hit.

But now, it was just me. No backup. No co-pilot.

Nice way to set yourself up for success, Kate. I seemed to keep stepping on rattlesnakes—literally and metaphorically. Meanwhile, Paul always had his headset on, mid-call, mid-deal, mid-something. The tracks were locked up. I couldn't remember my own street address.

There was a moment I just had to laugh at myself—like what even is this life?

And there was Will, my son, watching his mom try to adjust. The twins were thriving. The kids were all right. It was just me who felt like a glitch in the system.

I kind of let go of the idea of running historic Boston that year. That dream didn't fit anymore.

But here's the thing: I kept pushing through anyway.

And somewhere in the mess—in the rattlesnakes, the wrong turns, the fog of total disorientation—I had a breakthrough. Not the kind with finish lines and medals but the quiet kind. The kind that shows up only after you've lost your grip on everything you thought you needed to succeed . . . and kept going anyway.

So I forgot I had even signed up to be a participant in that one special October historic Boston 2021 Marathon.

Somewhere along those quiet, confused miles, I felt something shifting. Like the hard things of life—loss, major change, Covid, the move, the menopause fog, the starting over—were building something deeper.

Not speed. Not skill. But staying power. I went back East all by myself that October with no home there to stay at anymore. No Paul and none of the kids.

The October Boston Marathon took place on October 11, 2021—it was the 125th Boston Marathon and the only time in the race's 128-year history (as of 2025) that it was held in the fall instead of its traditional Patriots' Day slot in April.

The 2020 Boston Marathon was originally postponed due to COVID-19 and then ultimately canceled—the first full cancellation since the race began in 1897. Race day came. Cool air. October sun. I had run but not enough and with no real plan, just the belief that my body knew what to do, even if my brain felt a bit scrambled.

Then the rolling start? No gun went off, my run partner gave me a hug, and off we went. Despite thinking I'd feel jetlagged, weak, and unprepared, when I hit mile eighteen, something truly magical happened.

I wasn't at all breaking down. I was cruising. Flying. Like I could go forever. Stronger, faster, older than I'd ever been but lighter somehow. Freer. Like every hard mile—every lost run, every silent tear in the bathroom after another packing box, every "where the hell am I?" moment —had secretly trained me for this one glorified moment. It was almost impossible to feel this good on the back half of Boston, yet for me, on that one day, it was the ripple effect moment of my mile twenty-three.

Because it was not about running; it was about challenging past a comfort zone mentally, even if it felt wrong. It made me stronger, when I did not see it.

That's the secret no one tells you. The more times you hit it—the unraveling, the unknown, the "this is too much; I can't do this" mile— the better you get at walking straight into it. Smiling at it.

Sailing through it.

I finished that race the fastest I'd ever run Boston, feeling the best, and the oldest I'd ever been.

The most unsure I'd ever felt. And somehow . . . the strongest. Not because I trained perfectly. Not because the plan went right. But because I'd learned how to breathe through the chaos. How to trust the grit and grace built in every hard season before this one.

Mile twenty-three started back at age twenty-seven as an enemy; then it was the place where I knew exactly what to do. When the push doesn't feel like a punishment but a possibility. This will be the same for you too.

The beauty is sometimes in letting go of that control grip.

There are moments in all of us when our hands tighten around the known, as if it's the last rung on the ladder. Wise, planned, protected, and prepared.

But what you're really doing is bracing for a life or a race that's already moved on without your permission. Because when the unknown knocks, it never waits for your comfort. It doesn't care about your plan. You don't. You stall. You stiffen. You want order, control, and to build a life inside the muscle of resistance.

You say, "Not yet." You say, "Let me think about it." But what you mean is, "I'm scared." And that's okay. That's holy, even. But you can't live there. Fear will decorate your life in safety and silence until one day you look around and realize nothing's broken because nothing's moved.

And maybe the truth is this: Control is a comfort blanket sewn out of lies we were handed when we were young. "If you're good, you'll be safe." "If you plan well, you'll win." "If you know what's coming, you won't fall."

And sometimes, the most courageous thing you can do is lighten up, loosen your grip on the plan, on the pain, on the version of yourself that was always so certain, so tight, and so tired. Because there is something more honest waiting on the other side of surrender. Not safety but freedom.

Just as we settled into a bicoastal move, I felt off, unprepared, and shaky.

Then six weeks later: The foundation built for a decade proved me totally wrong.

For reasons I'll never fully be able to explain, I caught it. I will remember the light, crisp October air, the beautiful day to run Boston in fall colors instead of sunny spring bloom. I remember my post-Covid, hormonal body was so beyond unsure. It was stiff, rusty but willing now in my early fifties. I was jetlagged, had just had another knee surgery, a bicoastal move two months prior, and I was living in a rental home with bad sleep. I'd just winged it for a six-week training cycle with no track open. No gym. No weights. It made no sense to line up, but I loosened the control and had the experience of a lifetime.

I did remember climbing the fence of a track when my husband had just said everything was closed. And I just climbed right over the fence.

I was so annoyed by my husband because he was moving slowly. Everything was not possible. He handles problems differently than I do. He's a little more skeptical. I'm more "power through it, find a way." So what I thought was going to be taken care of by a relocation company and a smooth, concierge-style move turned out to be me hustling around L.A. while trying to adapt and get the kids acclimated.

That race will live inside me forever, not because of its result but because of how present I was. It was a teacher and reminder. *The Power of Now* was alive again. I remember the feeling at the finish, but because it was my fastest finish at my oldest age.

I was peaceful for a little over three hours. Despite the stress, the "adjustments," and opening my eyes, running isn't just about training, it's about being.

And sometimes, the best experiences aren't the ones you plan, score in, or dominate; they are just the ones you feel you're growing and happy in. They're the ones you survive beautifully. I will carry that day as long as I live because being "home" with all the extra challenges of not being a local anymore, I realized I could do that. It was not the A plan of familiarity but the B plan of giving up full control and still feeling gratitude and grace.

Stop Living Small

Maybe you're the practical, rational, logical type. The "what-if, what-not" person. The one who sees the cracks in the plan before the dream even begins. The empty side of the glass. The risk before the reward person. The fall before the climb. Maybe you've made your life smaller just because of that one habit of self-talk.

Maybe your cave is too tight. Your ceiling is too low. Yes, I see you because I have been there too.

Settled for safety, predictability, and practicality when you were meant for something bigger. I've been there too.

I've lived small because small felt safe. Because dreaming bigger meant risking failure, or worse, disappointment. Because it was easier to stay quiet than to speak up.

Are you prepared to leave comfort to reach a better place?

Easier to plan than to leap. Easier to manage expectations than to raise them.

But deep down—you know. You know just like I do, you're way more than that. You've always known that. You can break that inner doubt. I know you can.

That's when the visualization matters. That's why when you hit mile twenty-three—when you're empty, spent, unsure, broken—you have to see yourself bigger. See yourself taller. On many days, when time didn't allow and my mind and body were screaming, another voice said this: "If it is to be, it is up to me."

Shoulders up. Heart open. Soul wide. Picture the impact of the person you want to be. The person you could be. The person who belongs in a bigger space, in a better body than you've been living in.

And then, no matter what—find the way to get there. Don't say what if or make excuses. Crawl if you have to. Breathe into it. Manifest it. Take a photo. Take twenty. Make an album on your phone to refer to on your weakest days. Maybe it is the acceptance to an Ivy League college, a high school, a home, a bank account, a golf score, a trip you can't afford, a marathon finish line time, a boat, a summer house, or your unique dream all of your own.

Breathe if that's all you can do. But move. Make a plan and move mentally, then physically.

Because this is the real cost of mile twenty-three: not muscles. Not stamina. But the true and honest talk with yourself and your willingness to stop living small. The courage to become larger than your fear. To stand taller than your past. It's about what you're made of when you've got nothing left. Your will—the tiny, raw piece of you that refuses to die, will and should whisper, "Yes." And the magic, that impossible, holy magic, is what happens if you reach past both.

Past logic. Past comfort. Into the blind spot where there's nothing left but faith. A little more patience. A little more focus and a lot more honest surrender. That's the invisible cost of your own finish line. Not strength. Not confidence. But the last inch of soul you didn't even know you had. In the breaking. In unraveling. And in the quiet, stubborn choice to go anyway. The realest, most vulnerable thing any human can admit is in saying, "I quit. I want out." And something greater pulled me back in. Letting go of the outcome, doing it anyway, and the quiet, painful grace of finishing because your soul demands it, not for the medal, not for the time, not for applause. Just to keep on keeping on.

Finish What You Start

Letting go of that outcome and detaching from attachments might be a better race. The one that happens when you have no outcome to chase. When you're committed to finishing whatever goal you set for yourself, even if you get nothing tangible to your eye or soul out of it at the time, you'll be OK whether you win or lose. No joy in your legs. No fire in your heart. When everything hurts and you have every reason to quit. When it gets too foggy to see.

My brother Gerry, thirteen months older than me, passed away three weeks before the 2025 Boston Marathon. The last thing I actually wanted to do was run. I wanted to grieve. To mourn. To sit in my bathrobe on the floor and let the sadness have me. I wanted to be home, holding the pieces of what memories of life had just broken apart. After Gerry's funeral, the plans were already made. I got in a couple long runs —not because I felt strong but because a part of me didn't know what else to do. Moving forward, it was the only language I could still speak.

Both of my girls had a volleyball tournament in Salt Lake City the week before Boston; they both got the endo virus, which they passed on to me. I thought I'd dodged it, yet smack on Easter Sunday, the day before the Boston Marathon, I woke up with my eyes swollen shut and something brewing. When race day came, I stood at the start line a little empty. Gerry and his four amazing kids' photos were taped to my bib. I was bloated, puffy, and tired, with the enterovirus in my system. I told myself: Just be in it for Mathew, Andrew, Jed, Erin, and Christine.

Honor them. Think about their uphill road and pray to Gerry. It's okay if you don't finish. So after the national anthem, the gun went off, and I ran with the endo virus. As I got to Heartbreak Hill—where our house was—I stopped. Dead in my tracks. I ducked under the yellow tape, and I started walking home on the sidewalk. I quit. I've never quit in a marathon or race. This day, I did. I quit. I said to my brother Gerry,

"Please, just let me be done? I love you. I have you here with me, and I promise to be there for your kids, but my town burned down, I'm pissed you're gone, and I am real sick. Ger, I don't have anything to prove. I don't need a medal nor fast running times anymore, right Ger?" I walked slowly up that Heartbreak Hill, feeling the weight of him, the instincts and emptiness of quitting. Then I heard it. A voice—quiet but firm—deep in the place where the truth always waits: "Kate, get your ass back out there and finish what you started." See, my brother Ger, he was a no-nonsense grinder, and he was gone now. Gerry shaped me growing up. When he wanted it, he did it. No matter what. He was filled with warmth, humor, love, and intelligence. I heard him say, "We won't be having any of that today, Kate." Don't finish for the medal or for the time. Finish for the principles I showed you. Keep on keeping on. For the promise you made to yourself a long time ago: You finish things even when they feel impossible, even when they hurt, even when they break you. Even when they mean nothing. Even when no one is watching. So I did. Thanks to his voice.

I crossed back over the tape and gave the medal to my nephew. Got the chills, a low-grade fever, and went through two boxes of tissues that night, thankful for Gerry's voice and presence in my spirit.

That voice—the one that pushes you to keep going no matter what, no matter how hard—staying in it, finishing it, following through on what you committed to. That voice sticks with you, reminding you that outcomes don't matter. If your voice doesn't have it, borrow someone else's. The glory? Doesn't matter. The win? Doesn't matter. What matters is showing up, keeping on, doing what you owe yourself—a goal, a dream, a process. Because your real race begins the moment you promise yourself you will. Stay in it, stay with it, even when you're sick, the divorce wipes you out, the house is gone—you wipe those tears, get back up, see a new goal, and finish the vow you made to yourself. It will follow you if you commit to it. It will follow you sixteen years later. Like mine has.

Because when you let go of the outcome—when you run simply because you promised yourself that you'd keep running—that's when the real race begins. You know what I've learned?

It's never about whether you feel like you have more because you won't. It's about whether you're willing to reach into the blind vacant area, past logic, sense, and comfort—to pull out just a little more faith, a little more patience, a little more surrender.

That's your glory of your finish line. It's not the miles—it's that last inch of soul that you didn't even know was there.

The magic doesn't come from breezing through it. It comes from breaking—and still not quitting.

That was true, at least for me. Didn't believe that I was anything special. Still don't. But the magical moments I have experienced where I pushed past a threshold physically, mentally, and emotionally came from a deep invisible something in me—a tiny grain of sand—that said, "Hold on." A blind spot.

This might be the most important thing we can focus on while asking you about outcomes. Yes, it is natural to want a tangible outcome for most things in our lives. If I do X, I get Y. I want something tangible out of the effort for this. Run experts say this: For a person to break a 3:15 marathon time, you have to run a sub twenty 5K and a sub forty 10K. I didn't. I ran a 3:08 without that formula because I didn't attach to a formula. I just stretched the person inside to get there. I wanted an outcome for coming to California. My new mile twenty-three challenge is real.

Yes, I'm living in a beautiful place, California. But I'm also raising two daughters in a city of mirrors and filters, watching them take in mixed messaging wrapped in flawless packaging, trying like hell to just keep going with it.

Yes, this wasn't really the A plan. But it's where I am, and what's the point of living if you can't learn to live in the now, make the best of it, and adapt?

Comfort tells you to stay where you are because the unknown might hurt, but growth guarantees some pain. It's part of the ticket price.

You want transformation? Then you have to stop worshipping comfort and start courting discomfort.

16

SETBACKS, SUNSHINE, AND STARTING OVER

"Of all the people you will know in a lifetime, you are the only one you will never leave or lose. To the question of your life, you are the only answer. To the problems of your life, you are the only solution." —Joe Coudert

Sometimes, I feel like I'm planting seeds in soil I don't even understand. Hoping the sun, the rain, and the world will just be kind to them, even if I no longer know the seasons by heart.

The greatest healing has always come to me not just in the big, life-changing moments—but in the small, quiet acts of kindness, the kindness I give and receive.

Especially the ones that come from total strangers.

Parenting in California is already a kind of translation, but when you're navigating two cultures, it becomes a high-stakes interpretation of values, preserving roots, and learning when to let go.

L.A. has certainly gotten the last laugh on me. Just when I thought I was an expert at adaptation, change, flexibility, grit, and resilience, it was another wake-up call, just like the bombing in Boston was. It was a reminder not to take for granted our inner constitution, to sharpen skills that get a little too familiar and may go dormant. Because let me tell you, even when you think you have what it takes to handle them, think again.

Smiles seemed a little too perfect here. Faces and bodies too. Beautiful, yes. But self-consumed. Breasts and faces pulled up, eyes lifted without eye contact or sincerity. Nobody slowed down to look you in the eye.

Most drove fancy cars. Many had personal life coaches, plumped lips, mushroom adaptogen lattes, and more.

Here I was trying to just be me, waiting to hear somebody yell, "Kate, move ya cah!"

There is an irony in the beauty of California against the hollowness. Yes, you can feel inside it. Like it dazzles you but doesn't touch you. The California eye candy is real; there is so much beauty here, it almost breaks your brain.

Mountains against the turquoise Pacific Ocean meet the clear, navy, stunning sky.

The ocean melts into the horizon. Flowers bloom like they never knew a winter.

Sunshine sparkles so hard it makes you squint, even when you don't want to. It's endless.

Some days, it doesn't seem real.

Not in the way Boston was real. Not the way home feels in your bones.

Being a newcomer here, I say, Why do I keep comparing? It isn't humble. It isn't sarcastic. It doesn't ask where you came from or who your people are or what your soul is made of. It doesn't give a shit about your education, your peeps, or your roots.

It only sees you now, on the outside. That's the real funny part. I had to check myself at the door, thinking I had always made friends so easily. Not here.

You could be somewhat breaking a bit inside—feeling a bit sad, tired, lonely—and no one would ever know. Yet they would never know, as long as you shine on the outside. As long as you sparkle.

That is not me, I thought. How is a weathered, side-eyed, socially awkward menopausal mama from Beantown supposed to hear this from the relocation lady, "Well, you certainly look the part of the Pacific Palisades!"

And yes, I did feel privileged to be there. It is an absolutely stunning place to live. It's seventy-five degrees with crisp sunshine every day and no bugs. I literally kept tripping while walking around the town the first day we moved there. Rolled my ankles a bunch, tripped about three times. I was mesmerized, looking around and feeling in total awe of the topography and wildflowers.

Yet there were women jogging with umbrellas, wearing full faces of makeup, fake eyelashes, and weight belts with no sweat. Let me tell you: starting over here?

Those "bad voices" came right back in: "What is all this flash, trash, big rush, and bad manners of the shallow people and confusion here? For God's sake, these lightweights look and act like they are in high school wanting to be popular."

I thought I had mastered these voices, and they were gone forever. Yet my control grip was tight and reserves were low. The voice changed to what I did not expect. Judgy. Who the hell was I to judge a place I'd never been to? I usually always see the good in people.

The one line that's been my anchor was: "If it is to be, it is up to me."

Do you want a fuller connection with people in your new move? You want to belong? You want to feel seen, valued, rooted?

Keep trying, right?

I invited my twins' sixth grade class of moms over for a breakfast as a start.

I went to make a toast, introduced myself, trying to be funny, saying, "I'm Kate, fresh out of friends here. I may be a bag of trash for a bit, but nice to meet you all. . ." And they looked at me like, What?

Nobody laughed.

I cleared my throat, stepped forward like I was walking on stage, and said, "Hi, I'm Kate. I'm from Boston, so I still think this culture shock is more blinding than the sun."

One person laughed. One. The rest just stared at me, their polite smiles. Oh God. It was bad. The kind of moment where your face flushes before your brain even catches up. I wanted to dive headfirst into the fruit salad and hide. Instead, I stood there, clinging to my paper coffee cup like it was going to rescue me from the social ocean I had just belly-flopped into.

It wasn't the welcome I'd imagined. But it was real. And sometimes, that's all you get—reality.

Who would've predicted that in the middle of a global pandemic, when Paul's job changed, ETF business? While crossing a bridge built out of RV fumes, fire pits, and sheer survival instinct—one that would lead me straight to a place I swore I'd never end up? Los Angeles.

The one city I said, "No way" to. Firm.

A city I knew myself enough not to live in, not with two growing twin girls to shape.

So the woman who arrived that August day in L.A.? I didn't really recognize her. I didn't really like her either. She got a D for effort and an F for attitude.

Sadly, I knew all the right things to do too. I've done this before—the work, the sitting still in far harder times of much bigger adjustments, transitions with deep stress. My mile twenty-three needed a tune-up, a revisit, and a refresh with a different lens.

Let's face it, we can all be our own worst enemy when that mirror gets blurry. When you park your car by your own intention and choose to be angry or bitter?

That's when the self-honesty, the journal to yourself, does matter. The inner details, the little things, the self-care, the faith, and appreciation in tiny fractions—like being your own best friend—and the whole damn kit and caboodle matter.

Currently, winds and wildfires blew in to begin all over again. I am now discovering a "next chapter" with a town that just burned down and a home I can't live in for a few years.

Let's do it, mile twenty-three. I have my shoes laced up, my head up, my heart strong, and I am ready to rumble.

Let's run together now, hand in hand, footfalls in unison, breath-work calm, steady, because you, my friend, have invited me forward again—and this time I'm ready for it and ready to help others.

Starting over isn't about becoming someone new; it's about letting the spicy, scrappy, screw-it-let's-laugh version take center stage and show up exactly as you uniquely are. Wrinkles, ugly hair, wisdom, weirdness, and a bloody shoe all over again—seasoned and far stronger.

Maybe you have to find yourself in a new school, a new town, a new job, a new friend group, a new team. At any of our ages and stages, new beginnings are just part of the deal.

In transitions through life, it is OK to feel empty and shaken in the beginning, when every new person's face feels cold and insincere. It's OK to hide and retreat when you know what you need to refill your tank. It's OK to resent your husband when nothing seems to faze him.

At some point, you say this: The choice to be happy is all mine. And if you can't get there? Pivots definitely help. If one thing doesn't fulfill you, try another path.

If you feel fresh out of friends like I did, why not find the flowers? Why not create something new while you're looking?

A small piece of land was for sale next to the Spanish house we bought. It was an extra million dollars for just dirt and stairs. But I caught a vision in that unique slope side, which sat empty and neglected for fifteen years. It faced the emerald necklace of the Pacific Ocean. I asked five of my neighbors if they wanted to go in on it together, and my neighbor next door and I decided to split it.

Then after a year, the fun began—but not the way I expected.

Dirty nails, sweat on my face.

The yard sloped downward on a hill, a bit dangerous, the stairwell dating back 7,000 years. Movie sets had filmed on it. I wanted to make it special.

I bought a ton of books, knowing nothing about gardening. I went to work, learning about the clay-like soil, locals trying to outsmart the gophers who kept eating the brand-new baby roots—with maybe a little cursing.

The gardener came one last time and dropped me off an axe, gloves, clippers, and shovel. He shook my hand, thanked me for the business, and just like that, we exchanged roles. He left. That's what I did. These guys became my serious, unique friends every day—learning, studying soil, drainage, and propagating talk. Butterflies, bees, owls, worms, snails.

They became my first loyal buddies. I had no prior experience in working in the ground—"grounding," as they call it. It works! Every single day, for hours on end, including weekends, I was an extremely happy lady in a place that brought joy in the dirt—planting, pruning, watering, feeding. Tending to not just the yard but to this strange, fresh life I was trying to root and grow here in L.A.

Little by little, I slowly made roots of my own. My husband thought we'd maybe play golf, hire a gardener. Tried that. They'd say, "Oh ma'am, you don't want to get your hands dirty, do you?" After I heard that four times, I decided to get my hands dirty with my new fresh friends—bougainvillea, sage, salvia, California poppies, lamb's ears, olive trees, rosemary, lemon trees, blooming cacti, California lilac, jasmine, rocks, water fountains, and sparkling sun.

This has never gotten dull, tiring, or old.

It gave me exactly what I needed. Roots.

I developed a bond and relationship with the form of beauty that pays you back. It might even bring a following.

The butterflies, bees, and the natural ecosystem all came together like magic.

I'd be pruning trees, airing out roots, bringing back dead stuff in joy.

I was staying honest to myself, leaning into routine and structure. From that place, I found reliable, quality, kind friends.

Then, Santa Anas came in, blowing at eighty miles per hour on January 7, 2025, right after Paul toasted on New Year's to all seven of us embarking on another year in our beautiful home in Pacific Palisades, California.

2025: "This will be the best year of the century." Poof. Everything went up in smoke.

Literally. I swear to you, if it weren't for the two saints taped to my fridge —Padre Pio and St. Jude—the house wouldn't be standing. The angel on my deck somehow held, and the soil I worked for two years to enrich the garden? It all remained despite the fire. It climbed right up and over it.

Yes. There's armor, and then there's experience.

After enough battles, you start to recognize the pattern. *Life will interrupt you*, over and over again. Plans will unravel, and certainty evaporates.

Doors you thought were yours slam shut. But here's what no one tells you: that interruption, that inconvenience, that derailment—it sharpens your instincts.

It also teaches you super skills—the kind you don't learn in school. The kind that come from crawling through the cracks when the path gets blocked. You either shrink or expand to get through—but either way, you change. It's not just about me. It's not about me or my family; it's about everyone's family. In every challenge.

This is what it means to be human—right?

It's learning how to walk through the fire together and come out the other side—a little smoked, a little scarred, but still standing. You learn to adapt, pivot, rework, rebuild. You develop an inner GPS that recalibrates no matter how many wrong turns you take.

It's currently June in the Pacific Palisades. Perfect, sunny, breezy. The kind of day that makes this place look like paradise from the outside —clean sidewalks, ocean glittering below, the faint smell of salt and eucalyptus in the air. But no one says it out loud. No one says what they really want.

What everyone here aches for—quietly, secretly, like a prayer—is certainty.

A warm, solid hug from the god of knowledge. From Zeus himself, maybe—the only one strong enough to whisper, "It's going to be okay. You are safe. You will not be burned, shaken, or broken again." That Zeus kind of hug, connection, and friendship I felt years back in Nantucket from a man who did his work with his wife and faced his pain with every fiber of his being in just one hug, saying, "It will all be OK, and you will too." That kind of certainty and power from an old friend is what carries us in these moments.

Because no matter how perfect the sunshine feels today, every single person in this town remembers January 7, 2025. The day everything came undone and 35,000 people were forced to run. Evacuate. Leave homes, pets, photos, baby blankets, hard drives, wedding rings.

Fear moved faster than the fire that day. It wrapped around us all— tight, choking, no mercy—spitting chaos into every driveway, every canyon, every quiet street we thought we knew. I remember it like it was stitched onto my skin. The wind was hot against my face. The low growl of sirens cut through the canyon.

The endless line of brake lights creeped down Sunset Boulevard, every car packed with some stranger's entire life crammed in the back seat. It was perfect in its horror.

A day of fear so pure, so exact, I could feel it in the soles of my feet.

And now—even on a golden afternoon like this—there's a quiet hum of nerves under the beauty. A feeling behind the eyes of every runner, every dog walker, every mom pushing a stroller. Like maybe the earth could turn on us again. Like maybe the god of certainty is busy somewhere else.

But we pretend. We smile. We wear sunglasses and sip coffee and nod at each other like it's just another California day. Because here, you learn how to live with beauty and fear holding hands.

17

THE PALISADES WILDFIRES—CHAOS AND COMMUNITY UNITED

"When you know that you are capable of dealing with whatever comes, you have the only security the world has to offer." —Harry Browne

The Day the Fire Came

It started with a text from my friend Miranda.

"Get out fast."

No greeting. No emoji. Just those words. And then the emergency alert exploded on my phone—sharp, loud, blaring like the end of the world.

My whole body started to shake. Hands, knees, chest. My breath got stuck somewhere halfway up my throat. I'd been hiding in the garage—because I didn't want to see the wind. I didn't want to feel it pushing against the house, pulling at the trees, threatening the sky. If I couldn't see it, maybe it wouldn't matter.

Maybe the day could stay normal.

But it wasn't normal. I knew that when I opened my inbox that morning and saw an article I'd sent to my husband about conserving water—mindful water use—as if that mattered anymore. As if water would save us. And then it hit.

Black smoke, fast, low, and violent, was swallowing the canyon like some beast let loose.

No time for plans. No time for careful packing or lists or bags. I grabbed the dogs, my phone, my rosary beads. Opened the door. Felt the hot wind slap my face.

And I ran. No shoes. No coat. No keys or a bra. Not a suitcase, shoes, or bag.

Just me running down the street on bare feet, the pavement scraping, the air choking, the world turning to ash behind me. I glanced back once. Had to get Will, Lucy, and Riley.

The deck. The angel stood there, watching. Saint Jude and Padre Pio were taped to the fridge, holding their ground inside the house I was leaving behind.

God, this was rich and human and real.

Fear crashed into relief. Chaos bumped into normal life, disaster and family colliding in the weirdest, most unforgettable way.

I didn't even see that I didn't have a car. Let's start there with how our brains absorb shock. All I knew was I had two dogs, a phone, my rosary beads, and bare feet pounding the pavement as black smoke chased me down the hill. And then—like a dream breaking into real life —there he was. My son. Magical Willie Wonka, sitting in the car at the bottom of the street. Calm as ever. Smiling that smile that always says, "I've got this, Mom." Eating his Poké bowl. "Chill," he said to his mom.

The same kid who'd been curled up in pain just a day and a half before—a twisted testicle from sleeping wrong on the plane ride home after New Year's. We'd just flown back on January 5. Spent New Year's in the clouds, thinking the hardest part of the month was behind us.

But January 7 had other plans. This was his first real day out of pain. His first chance to get back to himself.

And here he was—grinning in the passenger seat like it was just another cool California afternoon—watching his barefoot mother run down the street, dragging two dogs and screaming about fire.

I must've looked insane.

And him—with his Poké bowl and that dimpled smile—cool, calm, collected as ever. But I could see it in his eyes. That little flicker of worry behind the grin.

He knew this wasn't right. I flung open the car door.

"We have to go! The whole street's gonna burn, the car's gonna burn, we're gonna burn!" I was yelling. Shaking. My heart was banging so loud in my chest I could barely hear myself.

And Will—steady as ever—just looked at me and said, "Mom, it's okay. Mom. . . we're driving away, and the dogs are still on the leash on the street. You shut the door. The dogs are still outside."

What? I looked down. Oh my God. There they were, Brady and Finn—standing in the street. Leashes dragging. Staring at me through the glass like, "Really, Mom? Seriously?" I almost drove off dragging them behind me.

I flung the door open, yanked them inside, clumsy and frantic, hands shaking, and right then—right in that perfect chaos—Brady threw up.

Poor thing. The panic in my body flooded into him. The dog vomited right there on the seat. My hands were still clutching the leash like a lifeline.

I climbed in. The dogs leapt over the seats. My hands shook on the wheel.

And somewhere, under all the panic, I thought:

God, how weird this life is. How beautiful and stupid and terrifying this moment is. My son with his Poké bowl and his quiet smile. Me barefoot and wild-eyed. The end and the middle of everything at the exact same time.

The Pacific Ocean had an unusual gray chop to it too.

11:11 on the PCH, Make a Wish

We peeled out and hit the PCH at exactly 11:11. I remember that. The numbers burned into the dash like some strange omen.

The palm trees along the highway were bent sideways, snapping and thrashing like they wanted to break free. The Santa Ana winds were howling at eighty miles an hour, stripping branches, ripping at signs, throwing dirt and debris across the road.

The air smelled wrong. Burning plastic. Ash. Something sharp and chemical, like the end of the world was dressed in gasoline.

I'd always had a healthy fear of the Santa Anas—the way they come fast and mean, stripping the canyon bare. But this? This was different.

I glanced in the mirror and saw the smoke boiling up, fast and dark, crowned with orange flames licking toward our neighborhood. Like the fire itself knew exactly where it wanted to go. Like it had decided to come straight for us. No time to think. No time to plan.

Some women had fire boxes ready—zippered cases full of documents, jewelry, baby photos.

Some stayed behind to tape windows, soak rags, defend their homes, waiting for that awful moment when the sky goes black and the world catches fire.

Not me. Not this time. My instinct was pure and sharp and wild: Get your people. Get your dogs. Get the hell out. Nothing else really mattered. The house, the things, the memories taped to the fridge. They could burn. So we drove. Fast. Wind was pushing against the car. Flames raced behind us. And somewhere in my mind, between the smoke and the smell and the fear, I thought: This is what it feels like when you stop caring about anything but staying alive.

As Will and I drove toward the California incline, the wind still howling, the sky thick and strange, I glanced in the rearview mirror. And I knew. I knew in that one quick glance—right there where the PCH meets the Jonathan Club—that this was probably it.

We weren't ever coming back to the Pacific Palisades.

Not like we were before. Maybe not ever. I took a slow breath.

I remember seeing these two men walking along the PCH as the fire raged in the distance. They weren't afraid—they were almost. . . excited. Hands in the air, grinning wide, like they were welcoming the chaos. Like they wanted the fire to come closer. It gave me this strange chill, like the world had flipped upside down, and no one was acting the way they were supposed to.

I held the rosary beads in my hand—cold and smooth and familiar—and I felt that little click of calm wash over me. It wasn't fear. It wasn't sadness. It was something else.

A deep, sturdy, unshakable peace. Like a quiet wildfire inside me was answering the one raging behind us. Because the truth hit me hard and clean, the way only *mile twenty-three truths* do: If our house slid down the hill, if it burned into the sea, if the photos, the papers, the shelves of memories turned to ash, I would still be standing strong, sturdy, and anchored. Will would still be beside me. We would keep going. Because I'd built something stronger than walls. A foundation poured from something tougher than wood or glass or steel.

Tertius cement. Stability laid two decades ago.

And no Santa Ana winds—no wildfire—could take that.

A tear slipped down my cheek. Small. Crocodile slow. But my hands stayed steady on the wheel. I glanced at Will. He looked at me. We both took another breath.

11:40 a.m.

We drove on toward Marymount High School.

The strength and certainty I felt in that moment was pure gold. Like being my own Zeus. Knowing I had what it takes to handle the type of mayhem, what I built from ashes fifteen years prior, brick by brick, slowly, carefully, gently, and in that moment, it felt like a spirit not even of my own—it was a blissful, unshakable calm. I don't handle small things as well as the catastrophes, but I was taking advantage of the current moment, as well as some satisfaction in hearing my Italian Stallion husband, Paul, sounding a little panicked on the phone.

He was sweating through his suit, sticking to the leather in his car on the PCH, thinking he could figure out how to get home.

As I drove past him opposite side of PCH, I couldn't help but grin and laugh under my breath. Mr. Smooth thought he could save the day, make it back to pack essentials, like the fire, the traffic, and the madness would somehow part for him.

He hadn't quite grasped the reality of the situation. I had, and despite educating him for two years on "Stop wasting water, have an emergency plan, and a fire suitcase kit," he'd blow it off, laughing at me, saying, "Kate, nothing has happened in twenty years."

So for a minute, it felt satisfying to feel an "I told you so" moment.

Mr. Calm, Cool, and Collected, sweating into his leather seat, sounding panicked. Me? Cool as a cucumber.

I was very sad for our community, more than I was for us, and very grateful my mom and dad got to see our town. After making a mindful point days earlier to have an emergency plan, again my husband laughed because I did not bother, just ran out and left without even a bra or shoes. Phone was ringing off the hook, texts were coming in, and everyone was panicked. I wasn't. Not at all. It was just the opposite. I truly knew with all certainty that I couldn't control what was about to happen, and I did not need anything except my calm institution and my people, and all the rest, I could let go.

I worried for our priest, our former school, close neighbors, and a small group of families, yes.

We arrived at my twin daughters' school around noon, and a group of girls came out wanting and needing hugs.

I went straight to the school chapel, not out of fear but out of gratitude to have the grace to give a hug like Zeus did for me and others. A peace came over me to the godmothers of my girls who had helped so deeply in this way years prior. To just "know," to cope, comfort, and help be a strong anchor for others is a light, a gift to pass on to my own family and friends. To unplug from that chaotic time frame of an hour or two.

Los Angeles became sheer and utter pandemonium. Information overload. I put my phone away. It was way too much to take in between the news, Nextdoor, group texts, and women (the home caregivers, emotions screaming through words). I had a locked-in security plan right inside my heart. Everyone naturally grasped for a sense of control. I couldn't control anything, so I chose to let it be.

Their free period was at 11:30 a.m., free periods being the time frame they are allowed access to phones. On that day, this did not serve any girl under the age of eighteen well. It was an all-girls, independent school; the kids were not all from the Palisades. It's a fairly diverse school. And it was girl-heightened fear and emotion. They were whispering to one another, getting the skinny on the severity of the fire. In seconds, roughly four hundred girls got this information overload. Then they went to emotion overload, with fear, tears, and panic. The school should have been notified to inform the girls before they got access to phones.

Some of them learned while standing in their uniforms during their free period—phones buzzing, neighbors calling, texts flashing: "Your house is on fire." Others pieced it together slower—word by word, whisper by whisper—as the news snuck down Sunset Boulevard like the wind itself.

The winds that day weren't normal. They didn't blow in just one direction.

They whipped east and west, south and north—wild, spinning, scattering flames like angry confetti—taking out whole streets, whole hillsides, whole corners of life. One teacher found out her neighborhood was gone before she finished grading her papers.

A coach heard his childhood church was burning down while lacing up his shoes. A family at our school lost the grocery store they shopped at every Sunday—the place their little girl first learned to count apples.

Sunset Boulevard became a funnel of smoke and heat—blowing fire across every familiar turn, every favorite coffee shop, every shortcut home. No warning. No time. Just quiet, fast whispers. . . "Did you hear?" "It's on fire." "It's gone. Gelson's is gone. Pali High too."

The whole town and community banded together, all in sync with one another, learning to let go in real time. The freshmen and sophomores all needed rides. The girls were hugging, crying, staring at phones. The juniors and seniors drove out, having cars of their own, not knowing where to go, how to cope, and calling Mom and Dad.

It was like watching a movie of emotions, seeing, feeling how it impacted all of them so personally. Their own life history as they knew it was going up in flames.

This was layered humanity—the ache of watching your child feel loss again—the past grief folding right into the present one.

The Same Tears

The only thing I trusted that day was the Fire Duty app.

No news station, no neighbor text, no guessing game of wind and luck. Just that little screen, that glowing ring of fire spinning, circling—closing in on our friends' homes, the girls' school, our church, our own neighborhood.

For hours, I watched it.

And strangely, after years of unknowns, after trauma, loss, fear, death, change, and beginnings I never asked for, this didn't feel strange. This not knowing. This waiting for the worst. I was okay. We drove. My girl Riley jumped into my car. Lucy into Paul's.

I looked over at Riley sitting beside me—pink face crumpled, tears spilling, her little chest shaking—and I knew that face. It was the same face she'd worn three years earlier, aged twelve, stepping off the plane from Boston to L.A., leaving behind her friends, her street, her whole world.

It was the face of grief. Of starting over when you don't want to. Of having no say in what you lose. Here she was again. Same tears. Different reasons. But this time, the grief wasn't old familiar sidewalks and snow-covered mailboxes—it was her sixth to eighth grade school, her church, her places with her buddies, her memories of the life we had just built.

I felt a little squeeze in my chest, the quiet helplessness of a mother who could not fix this one. She wiped her face fast, like she always does. Grabbed a tissue. Cleared her throat.

"Can we go to Manhattan Beach, Mommy?" she asked softly.

"That's where all my friends are." Twelve years old again at that moment, going on sixteen all at once. Looking for home. Again.

I just reached for Riley's hand. Held it quiet. Held it steady. "It's all gonna be okay," I said. And I meant it. Somehow. We wound our way into the heart of downtown—the Financial District of L.A., landing in a hotel room on the top floor. Strange and high and far away from everything familiar. Dinner came to the door. Prosecco too. Like a reward for surviving the day.

That night, I opened the curtains and stood there in the dark, staring out across the city.

And there it was. The loud orange glow of fire, still growing, stretching its terrible fingers across West L.A., curling toward Hollywood, to Pasadena, and traveling to places nobody would have expected.

Places I thought were safe. The blaze wrapped the city like a crown of flame. It didn't even feel safe to get a wink of sleep. A few hours passed. The clock moved slowly and uselessly.

At 5:30 that morning, when the sky was supposed to soften, when the light should've come, I opened the curtains again, and the entire sky was still black.

Thick black. Ash black. Like the sun itself forgot to rise. Twenty, thirty miles in every direction, a lid of darkness sealed around us. The sun was up somewhere but not for us.

It was like watching the end of a movie that hadn't been written yet. And I stood there, holding the glass in shock, waiting for a sign of morning to break through. It never did.

After the fires swept through, we had to take it . . . just one slow day at a time. Too many decisions all at once were feeling quite draining for me, so I just went to church a lot and tried to stay at peace.

In every lobby of every hotel, looking at all the people's faces. Comparing notes. "Your house burned down?" "My house burned down too." Everybody looked dazed, confused, sad, and shocked. Each soul tried to help another.

The stores were giving out discounts. Mom friends from school had dispensary trunk shows of donations. So did the school. Free food here. Free mattresses there. Everyone scrambled to gather anything they could while they could.

Me? I couldn't really get my act together to do any of that. I was just trying to figure out the address of where I was and where I was going next.

There was a true comfort in being all together. Keeping the faith. Noticing. Listening. Comforting.

Trying to learn something from the fires. Trying to make meaning of it all. So of course—what do I do?

I put my sneakers on. The BAA had sent me two huge boxes of sneaks and clothing, so I began running. Training for the bib I'd earned last year for this year's 2025 Boston Marathon. Ironically, the playlist I made over Christmas to get "fired up"? I'd picked "Burning Man" by Dierks Bentley. And "Fire" by Brett Eldredge. I guess my subconscious mind was playing a trick on me over Christmas.

One hotel. Then another downtown. Then a hotel in Manhattan Beach. An Airbnb for three weeks, Palos Verdes for three weeks, and then another hotel in Beverly Hills for eight days. All just to find a rental. A lease for a year. Confusion? Oh, yes. Just a tad bit. My girls have been unreal, wonderful, strong, and resilient, not missing a beat. They do have to take a bus to school that is twice as long now as they did before.

It's hard to think about yourself when everybody else is sad and falling apart around you. It has certainly been an interesting time of reflection.

The night of the fires, the Santa Ana winds circled our neighborhood, whipping up and down the street, toward the ocean, back to the mountains, left, right, and sideways.

The fire began burning in the backyard. It hopped up blazing hot, fast, and furious—right behind our hill into the backyard. Somehow, it leapt over the house and set the front yard on fire.

I had to let it all go. Our front yard and hedge of privacy fig trees were on fire and spreading, then bam! Cort, an angel disguised as a fireman, stayed back with a hose to protect his people. That's the only reason our house really is still standing. The windows and door sealant all broke, so the interior allowed major smoke, ash, and water damage from the rains that followed.

Belongings inside the home all got ruined with extensive damage. Although we've lost a lot, the real important things remain. The people. Another angel showed up at the front door, fire surrounding the house, to get our photos, wedding rings, and passports.

The stunning, gorgeous hillside garden that we worked hard on for two years. Twenty hours of work weekly. Hands-on. Hands in the dirt. In the ground. Every day. Every single day, without pause, for hours, I tended to what we created. My little babies. Lamb's ears. Rosemary. Bougainvillea. Lavender. They had personality, history, purpose, and all our handprints on them. They also brought the butterflies, hummingbirds, and bees back to what was just a neglected pile of dirt with a set of ancient stairs that dated back to the Chumash tribe.

Ancient Stairs

The ancient stairs on the land I bought dated back to the Chumash Indian tribe. The planting around the stairs was all by feel and became my artwork. It was my idea and a labor-intensive job, which I recruited my kids and Paul to help with many a weekend. One day, with the axe, I said, "Paul—the stairs go way down further." And he said, "No, they don't." I said, "Yeah, they do." Lucy picked up the axe and said, "Mom's right, Dad. She found it."

We had a sitting area next to the volleyball court that covered the base of the stairs—and one day I could just picture it, feel it, and had to see it. Handmade tribal steps that extended down another twenty feet and left and right walls made like an amphitheater. That's where the Native American tribes all gathered seven thousand to ten thousand years prior. Sometimes, I'd go out in the backyard and pretend I was a Native American. Barefoot in the dirt. Sneaking between the trees, quiet like they must have been. Listening for animals. Touching the plants like they were medicine or food. I'd crouch low behind rocks, like I was hiding, waiting, watching. I'd even imagine what it felt like to live right there—no house, no cars, no noise—just sky and earth and fire. Sometimes, I'd dig in the dirt and find old things. Broken pieces, maybe from long ago. It felt like the past was still alive, right under my feet. Smelling the earth. Paul thought I was so strange.

The lemon trees, olive trees. All the flowers. The cracks of light were coming down—each lived in such harmony with one another. It was an education. Watching how they climbed. What direction they grew. Where they leaned.

It's no wonder that the garden is still beautiful right now. My neighbor, a chemist, found it a little funny that I was constantly talking to things in the backyard, but she and I had split the land together, and she has grown to love me. She saw and understood how much work and pride I took in it. Every inch of it. A space for Mom, for Andrew Morey, and for Jack Murphy. It all meant something.

Our street, Tramonto, means "sunset." They used the stairs for tribal gatherings, and the full amphitheater is covered. Later, they were used for movie sets, which is why I bought the land. I wanted something interesting. History in L.A. is not as easy to find.

Because that garden—I worked the hardest on it and loved it the most. I could have lived outside in a tent. It made me feel rooted here. And it's not by accident. Those saints on my refrigerator, souls planted in it, are spared. What I loved and put into the Earth—I'm sure of it. Right in the middle of that mess, Paul's dad had a stroke. Just like that.

As soon as Paul returned from being with him, it was time to pack again—no plan, no real place to land. Just knowing that we couldn't stay. And then Grace showed up.

Not the kind you pray for—the kind you meet. A lovely, special woman I had met a few months prior. She had a Harvard hat on. She, whom I barely knew, opened her beautiful home to us in Palos Verdes for three whole weeks. No questions. No hesitation. Just care.

I was truly and utterly stunned by the quiet, fierce outpouring from this L.A. community—the real one underneath the gloss. It was outlaw care. The kind that breaks rules and ignores lines. The kind that holds you when you've got nowhere else to go. Looks like L.A. got the last laugh on me and my wrong assumptions about it. It has just as much heart as Boston does.

I am still truly struck by the outpouring of love and care, not just from friends but from strangers. From this strange, sprawling city that I never thought I'd like or would feel like home. Los Angeles has gotten its last laugh because it's wrapped its arms around everyone, including us, in a way I never expected.

Manhattan Beach

While the layers of uncertainty kept piling up, life still had to move forward. Trying to put in miles for the Boston Marathon was not easy. Somewhere in the middle of it all, trying to catch my breath for one small moment of normal, I sat down with two girlfriends for a "let's take a moment" dinner.

A glass of wine. A yummy steak. A little peace with girlfriends in this delicious, swanky restaurant in Beverly Hills. Flowers, candles, and delectable wine.

And right there, starving as I took a bite of steak, my back molar cracked in half and broke cleanly off.

Of course, it did. Timing is an art and a science.

The next day, I was in the chair for oral surgery under general anesthesia because, apparently, even your teeth know when your life is falling apart. It was like living on cruise control through chaos—two months of scrambling, hunting for new leases, trying to anchor something steady when everything was sliding sideways.

But weirdly . . . deep down, I knew it would all be okay.

I have been here before—on the edge of the unraveling—but this time I knew I could hold on.

Because this mile twenty-three I was built for.

It's the little things that make everything better.

Like the kind, fun, and cool people in the city of Manhattan Beach who fully welcomed a town of strangers with wide-open arms, warm blankets, quiet kindness.

In one of our VRBOs, I remember hearing a soft thud at the front door. When I opened it, there were a few big trash bags full of clothing just sitting there. No note. No explanation. No name.

To this day, I have no idea who left them. And then there was my good old friend down the road—the one who became a kind of real-life Mrs. Claus. Every single day, she showed up. Sweatshirts, stuffed animals, a couch. More things than I could count. More love than I knew how to hold.

We never really know how good human beings can be until the world grays.

Crisis does that. It peels back the layers. And what's left—if you're lucky—is grace in human form. We never know how good human beings are until a crisis. Packages, cards, and care packages filled with sneakers and clothing. Being a non-collector and happy with a bare-bones closet, it was so shocking to me how women want to help other women. I was thinking peanut butter, PJs, running clothes, face wash, and toothbrushes. Everyone else had an abundance of things needed.

The families, faces of the struggling, the lost and scared, were familiar territory for me.

I feel deep compassion for the long-time Palisadian folks, the ones with a long history there; it's heartbreaking seeing them this sad. The kids are losing their schools and friends, and middle school and high school are being taught online. Older people are losing the history they so deeply loved.

I kept picturing that same fire in places like Newton, Massachusetts, or Scituate, and seeing my mom and dad lose the only history they'd known. Or me, seeing the city of Boston burn down and how much more impactful that would've felt. I don't have the same history my community did in the Pacific Palisades, and it's taught me a lot. Seeing them now was like looking at myself three years prior.

Temporarily losing our home wasn't half as gut-wrenchingly hard for me as it was for some of my friends and neighbors. I've gotten skilled at making a home within myself and fully understanding that whatever the trauma, death, and fears are, they will keep coming, and I am strong enough to handle them.

My suspicions about how poorly operated and dysfunctional Los Angeles was at that time were confirmed by the way the fires were handled. No water in the reservoir. No water pressure? Fire department cuts—in an area notoriously known for wildfires. On a windy, dry day. High alert. Where was the planning? Where was the thinking ahead of time? I never voted for the current mayor; there she was on the news, trying to cover her tracks while she was a foot out the door in another country. Nice. Thanks!

My son took his bike with a friend from South Bay back to the Pacific Palisades the day after the fires. He spoke to the firemen, whose station is at the bottom of our street. They said, "Son, your whole neighborhood should and could have been saved." All men in unison, shaking their heads in disappointment and grief, said this: "Your neighborhood especially could have been all spared if we had the water we needed." I could see it—my mother's hairy eyeball. Her spirit from heaven, a pause, a knock on Gavin Newsom's office door, a clearing of her throat, tip of her glasses, saying, "How in God's name did you let this happen . . . Aaaaaasswhole."

18

A LETTER TO MY PARENTS

There's a reason I still hear her in my head today. She's in the rocks, the ocean, the pauses. In the restraint and the hairy eyeball, the body mannerisms, the licking of lips, in the knocks on a countertop, and the flick of a wrist while skipping rocks.

Mom showed me that devotion and grace aren't weaknesses. Showing up quietly for the people you love, day in and day out, is one of the most powerful things any woman or man can do.

Especially when she did not have memories of her own mom.

Mom would say, "Be a friend to someone who doesn't have one today." "If you don't have anything nice to say, don't say it at all." "Sit up straight." "Go out and enjoy God's fresh air."

She helped with special needs kids. She was kind. She was a teacher. She always had compassion for people less fortunate.

And she showed that by her daily actions in how she cared for others. The cleaning man, the lady who came to polish our silver. The workers on the street.

Mom came from kindness, intelligence, and privilege. She had class. She was regal—in her own little way. My mother asked for very little. She gave a lot. She gave of herself all the time.

She showed up on the sidelines for everything—quietly, steadily, gently—never asking for anything back. If she got upset, she'd clear her throat, adjust her glasses, and say, "Excuse me," to make her point.

And when we were little kids, she never yelled like I do. She'd pick up laundry with her toes and zip around the house quickly and happily.

My older two siblings were extremely smart and high achievers. They were driven and accomplished. Then there was me. My mother never tried to compare me or pull me up the ranks to reach them. She loved the way I was—just the way I was. She used to smile, laugh, and get a kick out of me. She loved my boyfriend in high school and the cast of characters I hung out with. She admired my strong chicken legs, rubbing them all the time.

When Dad would say no to a social plan, I'd hear her always say, "Daddy, no, let her go, please let her go. She's a good kid."

I made a track in my backyard, ran in circles, did Jane Fonda, and worked three jobs every summer. While the five other siblings did golf programs, swim teams, and tennis, it was probably refreshing for Mom to just let me be, chew bubblegum, tan in the yard, eat my box of Raisin Bran every morning, and walk around with ankle weights to bulk up my chicken legs.

She totally let me off the hook. She rubbed the chicken legs, knowing someday they'd take me places she knew but I didn't. That's called wisdom.

My mother's uncle was a priest who baptized my sister in our family room. I remember being four years old, seeing my mom love my little sister so deeply as a tiny infant in a blanket and a blue bassinet, like she had no other children. That warm, loving face was special, and I will never forget it. My great uncle got Alzheimer's very early on, and sadly, that gene was passed right down to my mom.

As she began to go down that path, she became quite funny, and it was not immediately apparent. What we noticed is she would very gently—almost under her breath—whisper, "Asssshole." All the time. Two words, under her breath.

You'd have to be close to her physically and emotionally for her to even have the courage to say it.

She never swore; we were never allowed to swear in our house.

I remember saying to Paul the day we decided to go to L.A., "What if my mom gets sick?" Mom made it to the Pacific Palisades. And even as she declined, she was extremely lovable. The swears were beyond hysterical.

She even called me an "asshole"—but then she'd kiss my hand and laugh.

I flew home as much as I possibly could. Spent the summers there with her. And I was so grateful for that.

That loss—I didn't see it coming. It was a lot.

Flying east for college squash tournaments. Two college graduations. Middlebury, Colby. Holiday configurations on both coasts. Family. The logistics of getting Will off to college and graduating Loyola. I had to string it all together—like a chef on a shoestring.

The sooner we accept that part of living is preparing for storms and dancing in the drizzle, the better off we'll be because the truth is that it's never going to stop coming, but neither are you.

When you have to live far from home, you become a time traveler. You fill the birdseed with the hands that still remember your mother's. You swing a golf club and hear your brother and father's laugh playing in the wind like a half-forgotten song. You learn that grief doesn't just weep—it plants and grows.

I lost my brother and my mother in the last two years while living all the way across a country. Not a day goes by that I don't feel their absence in a thousand invisible ways—but I don't sit in sadness anymore. I can't.

The garden that I moved from pots on a roof in a home not safe to live in is now in sliver back patio recreated in South Bay. It's close enough to the Pacific Ocean that I can skip the rocks that say Nana, Mom, and Maitzie. There, in the garden and the ocean, between the olive tree and the sand, I keep a space where all memories can breathe. I made a space for them—not to hide my sorrow but to show what love looks like.

It's painted in colors they'd both appreciate. Gold for my mother's light. Indigo for the depth of my brother's spirit. A streak of wildfire orange because we're all a little scorched by this life, and still, we bloom. Sometimes, I see them in the birds, the hummingbird that hovers just long enough to say hello, or the song that comes on. This isn't sadness;

this is spiritual endurance. This is how I carry them—not as weight but as wind. I can't go back to where they are, but I can bring them forward with me. So I do. Love, when it's real, doesn't die. It just changes homes.

Whatever faith you have, whatever form it takes—there's no denying that some things in this life are just beyond coincidence. I don't always see it coming, but I always feel it after, whatever version of that steady hand, that invisible anchor, exists in our lives because it does take our strength to surrender to it. It takes courage to say, "I can't handle this." But when you trust in what you can't see, something unseen rises to meet you.

Faith is picturing that finish line even when you're crawling, even when your knees are scraped and your lungs are on fire, even if you fall flat—you still see it. You still fully believe you'll get there, and that's what faith really is. Not certainty. Not perfection.

But believing in the destination—before you ever arrive. *Spiritual endurance*. The muscle you build by living, not by wishing. If someone had told me fifteen years ago—when my boys died—that I'd someday be holding two little girls, I don't know if I would've believed them. Maybe I would've made it through those darker days a little faster. Maybe not. Grief is greedy. It doesn't care about your future. It just swallows your present.

And if someone had pulled me aside before Ryan's third heart procedure—the one before he collapsed on a squash court with a blood clot—and whispered, "It's going to be OK," maybe I would've exhaled a little deeper.

But by then, I'd already started to learn that it's always going to be OK. Not perfect. Not painless. But OK in the way that matters. In the way that lets you keep loving forward.

Because life isn't safe. Kids break bones. Accidents happen. You spend nights pacing floors, praying fevers down, and cursing the ceiling. But there's this kind of faith that comes—not the kind you perform in pews or wrap in quotes but the kind you earn in the furnace. Spiritual endurance. The muscle you build by living, not by wishing.

And that endurance, that resilience—you pass it down. Not like a birthright but like a shared secret. Your kids watch you rise, watch you cry, watch you laugh at the edge of total despair—and somehow, they learn to do it too.

That's the legacy. Not perfection. Not the right school or the right friends or gluten-free lunches. Just the faith that you can keep going. Even when you've got no map. Even when you're bleeding from the knees. Even then.

Especially then.

To anyone in the trenches: You're holding the line. You are doing holy work in the chaos of the everyday. You are carrying invisible loads that no one else can see, and your mindset is the map. Your energy is the current. Your belief—your quiet, stubborn belief—is sometimes the only thing that keeps you standing between survival and sinking. So keep going, even when it's ugly.

My Dad: "The Quiet Champion"

He is a man who taught without preaching and raised us by showing up.

My dad never gave long speeches. He didn't throw around big theories or read parenting books. He just walked through the door every single night at the same time, kissed my mother on the cheek, checked the sign-in sheet, and made sure we were all staying out of trouble. He was just steady, consistent, sensible, and stable in a world that's always turning itself inside out. That kind of steadiness was comforting and very holy as a kid.

To this day, he holds the longest-standing club championship record at the Hatherly Country Club. That record's held longer than some marriages but not his—she was a fifty-seven-year love of his life. I was his caddy. Well, "caddy" is generous. He never made it about his golf; it is pretty cool to see his name on the wall plaques year after year after year. I was a crappy caddy; he wanted me to just try to stay out of trouble at night and maybe earn enough tips. But out there on that grass, listening to the crunch of his golf spikes on the path, I learned a whole different kind of lesson. He'd talk me through each hole in a calm, measured voice: "Killer." He was my softball coach, and his nickname for me was Killer. I was a skinny, scrappy kid who hit softball hard enough for a home run to earn that name—"I'm gonna hit this here, then chip, sink my putt, and I will meet you at the next T-box, capisce?"

Simple, one, two, three. And then he'd actually do it. Always. He would make it seem so simple. Just get a two or a three on any given hole, confidently and intentionally. Then he'd just walk on, no theatrics, no drama. Dad was a player and a stud but never showed it. He never hung around. He played, came home, helped Mom, went grocery shopping, cooked, gardened, gave us a bath, and grilled dinner after shooting a sixty-seven for eighteen holes. I didn't really understand as a kid how cool that was.

Just quiet execution and a whole lot of presence.

That's how he raised us too. He had no father of his own to show him the ropes, but somehow, he built the whole damn tent.

Kept it upright, kept us inside. Didn't matter that I was sort of the oddball, the one who didn't look like anybody else. I didn't act or feel like anyone else either. I was sort of the wild card in a full deck of structure, but he let me be. Even when he didn't get it, he let me be. He had this line he'd throw at me when I went full glam, full blast:

"The package doesn't always look like the present, Killer." Which, let's be honest, was probably his silent way of saying: "Take off the purple eyeshadow." But what he meant was deeper. He was really saying: "Don't get tricked by the outside."

Know your worth, even when it doesn't match the label. Don't shrink and don't change for anybody. He taught me to stick to my guns. To trust my gut. If the boyfriend was causing conflict, he'd say another bus was coming along. You know what you're doing. To hold my faith and my priorities in check. That builds a girl's confidence. He helped everywhere possible.

You don't need a loud voice to lead a loud life.

Sometimes, you just need a good pair of golf shoes, a kiss at the front door, and a daughter watching every move you make.

Thanks, Dad. Raising six kids within eight years, including the teenage mischief years, got away from Dad. He would leave us a sign-in sheet for after dark. He tried to go to bed, reign us in, me in particular, but no, I was going out every night and dating a city boy. There was no way he was gonna tell me that I couldn't go on Spring Break my senior year in high school. So I earned the money to go, and I went. I won him a free trip while I was in Bermuda. They picked a girl and a boy off the crowded Elbow Beach in 1988, crowned them Bermuda Beach King and Queen, and gave me a free trip back, including hotel and airfare, which I gave to him.

P.S. I got away with it, Pops, just like you!

19

THE WILD ONES

My son, Will, as a three-year-old, bundled in his yellow slicker in London, rode in his red Bugaboo stroller. Every single day on the corner of Hyde Park heading to Green Park, a school bus would pass us, and in the window, the driver would spot him out of a crowd of people, point, and say, "That boy. That boy. He's got the beat!" And he'd stick his arm out of the window, smile big, and laugh like, yeah man, I see you! Will thought he was so unusually funny, being picked out of a crowded park every day. Will had and still has this magnetism that all strangers and people have felt. The beat that was built for him. At some point, as moms, we have to honor it versus squash it down. This spicy boy was the one whose magic and surprises had no end. He was the toddler who innocently flicked a pebble for fun, cracking his fair share of windshields. Naughty, funny, and expensive. He's the same one who snuck out the door after midnight as a freshman, took an Uber while I was asleep to go see a girl, got a ride back, texted a note to the parent from my bedroom and deleted it, all while Mum was nighty-night. I woke up and had no idea.

I'm sure everyone has that one friend. The one you love but quietly worry about. The one you have to think for—because they don't always think for themselves. The kind of person the angels stay busy watching.

I've got one of those too. The kid who once dove off a broken balcony into the freezing Boston Harbor, right under splintered docks and jagged beams—somehow landing twenty feet below without cracking his skull. The same kid who biked down Route Nine alone at four o'clock in the morning. For no reason. Just to see if he could. These stories are like little locked boxes in the attic of my mind. Old history. Same mischief. A fanfare of admirers followed him everywhere, half in awe, half wondering how the hell he was still alive.

We all know someone like that. The ones who test their own limits like it's a sport. Like the rules of gravity, time, and common sense don't quite apply. And they usually get away with it.

It's hard to stay mad at that kind of mischief. Yes, sir, as exhausting as they are to parent—the lectures, the warnings, and the shaking of the head—if I were not his parent, it would still be impressive. The sheer nerve of it. The boldness. The risk-taking brain that never stops inventing new ways to bend the rules, break the mold, dodge the ordinary. Way ahead of their years.

Too clever for their own good, maybe.

But funny as hell. The kind of cunning that you secretly admire, even as you're threatening to take away the phone, the bike, the freedom. Deep down . . . you know they'll probably make it in this world. And maybe even change it.

But what you're really doing is dimming a fire that was never meant to be safe.

These wild ones—their joy, their courage, their bigness—they're supposed to burn bright. To stir things up. To stretch what's possible. And sure, they'll make you crazy. Break the rules. Scare the hell out of you. They teach us something we lose as adults: fun, magic, spice.

Will came into this world as spicy, full-flavored, with an extra jalapeño and a side of sauce; he has magic in his every step.

Where there's a Will, there is a way; don't tell him what to do.

He's the kind of kid who doesn't just march to his own drum—he builds the damn drum out of broken rules and pure imagination. By teenage time, the world tried to shrink him. Sit still, be quiet, don't say that, don't feel that.

I don't want that, don't smile, don't laugh, and I want to see you cry and tell you to grab a tissue on the way out. Squish. The subtext of all that "too much" is just inconvenient for adults who forgot how to relate and feel.

But let me tell you something: When you squish the Wills of the world, they don't disappear, nor implode; they learn to wear a different mask, becoming a shell of a kid who's secretly screaming on the inside, unsure of whether the fire inside is a gift or a problem.

That's the true heartbreak of it all. That fire, intensity, and refusal to follow the script certainly can teach us all something. What if instead of breaking the stallion, you ran beside it? What if instead of telling a kid to be "less," you showed him how to use all that more for something honest, something beautiful, something real? You don't squish that kind of soul. You learn to hold it without holding it back.

That demeanor and fun are skills we all need for life. He gained an edge by age two. How to easily win people over and influence them does not always come in black-and-white form; it is in the invisible.

20

THE ART OF TIMING

Cleverly stitched onto my kids' ankles is our family's Roman numeral lucky number seven. A quiet little charm wrapped around their skin, holding some messy, beautiful history.

Moving to another country from 2007 to 2009 during the financial crisis, hmm, brilliant timing, right?

Or after ten years of asking, I finally said yes to L.A. in 2022.

Taking a year to pick a town, buying land, putting roots down, and right as we feel settled, finish the projects . . . poof! It all gets wiped away. Yes, timing, I guess, is everything. Losing homes. Losing lives all in conjunction with taking a risk.

Yet, somehow, not losing myself or perspective because the timing of it all can also be seen a different way. Look what is gained when things are seemingly lost: your mental strength, new people, new places, new discoveries, new mysteries, new faith, new belief, new healing. The good stuff. The seeing through the smoke, ash, deaths, grief, and feeling strong.

That? Keep the bad timing coming because I have way more to see, write, discover, and grow. We all do. And if you look around closely enough—really look—you'll see the signs too. The lucky sevens. The quiet winks. The reminders that this life is meant for more than safety and certainty.

It's meant for mile twenty-three. I don't know about you, but do you ever glance at your phone—11:11 staring back at you—and you pause, just for a second, and make a quiet wish?

Maybe it's silly. Maybe it means nothing. Or maybe numbers have more power than we give them credit for, little signals, little winks from the universe. Duality. Patterns. Timing. If I had met my husband in college, I probably would've overlooked him—too young, too distracted, too sure I knew what I wanted.

But life delivered him later, when I was paying better attention.

Paul listened.

He *cared*.

He actually gave a shit about what was going on *inside* me.

And that was new at the time.

The more I was around him, the more I felt like myself.

Like peas and carrots.

Like this is what love should feel like—not fireworks, but *firewood*.

Something that lasts. Paul stuck in my mind like a good song.

Once we were in, we were *all in*.

We golfed.

We skied.

We rode motorcycles.

We dirt biked.

We worked.

We partied.

We went to concerts.

We did drugs (yes, we had *fun*).

We were free.

It was real fun.

No pretense.

No pressure.

Just *partnership*—in all its messy, youthful, heart-forward glory.

I *knew*.

I *knew* I was going to marry him.

They say love is about finding someone who can skate on thin ice with you.

But real love?

Is finding someone who will dance on it.

Paul skated.

He danced.

He laughed.

He steadied me.

And even now—through the grief, the chaos, the fire, the healing— he is still *my person.*

The man who met me at the surface of my soul and stayed there, hand in hand, long after the music changed. Timing.

To be honest, some days I hear life whispering: *This isn't going to be easy, friend. But it will be real interesting.*

Sometimes, it feels like the numbers and the timing, and the patterns aren't on my side.

But maybe they are, and maybe they always were.

Maybe the point is to notice them. If you roll the dice, pay attention to the timing.

The perfect, invisible, effortless timing that happens every single day without applause.

The timing of the coffee on my nightstand—hot, strong, waiting for me because somehow my husband knew I'd need it before my feet even hit the floor. Or the timing of getting into my car late for a meeting and seeing the battery fully charged—because he thought to plug it in the night before.

Good timing.

February 2020

Just as I was pulling into Middlebury—armed with snacks, tissues, and every ounce of maternal wisdom I could summon—to console my daughter over some boy troubles (because heartbreak doesn't care if it's midterms week), the school broke out in COVID.

Campus lockdown. No visitors. Hugs through car windows. I'd

barely opened the trunk before I was back on the road, sympathy still warm in the passenger seat.

Meanwhile, back at home, the world was unraveling. After thirty years of marriage—thirty—I'd occasionally toss out the idea of camping to my husband. "Wouldn't it be nice?" I'd say, picturing lakeside mornings and trail mix under the stars. He'd just laugh. Paul doesn't camp. Paul books T-times.

So imagine my surprise—no, my shock—when I pulled into the driveway that day, and there he was. My husband. The man who doesn't even like folding chairs. Pulling up in a camper. A big ol' RV, parked like he was auditioning for a crossover episode of the *Partridge Family* and the *Brady Bunch*.

Right at the start of COVID. No warning. Just . . . there.

"Figured we might need it," he said with that grin that meant both everything and nothing.

He was ahead of the plan. I didn't even have a plan. But there he was —with wheels, a kitchenette, and the strange calm of someone who'd decided that maybe, just maybe, adventure was our new survival strategy.

So we camped. Not because we were ready. But because he showed up. And sometimes, that's what marriage looks like: decades of saying "no," until one day, the world falls apart—and the answer is suddenly, wildly, beautifully yes. Who could ever plan for this one: the whole world freezing for COVID and my husband pulling into the driveway with an RV? No roadmap. No answers, yet it was the exact thing we needed to keep moving forward when the world told us to stop.

We wheeled from Hershey, Pennsylvania, to Williamsburg, to Pinehurst, to Charleston, South Carolina, to Hilton Head, North Carolina. And one more, winding up in a parking lot at Pinehurst prestigious golf course . . . because of course we did.

And did we stop to rest? Not really. Boys stopped to play eighteen holes. Because sometimes, the best detour is the one that makes zero sense at the time. That trip wasn't curated, color-coded, or even particularly sanitary, but it was alive. That's what made it unforgettable.

The truth was there wasn't a better alternative.

The entire country had just shut completely down, remember? We just kept driving south, outrunning lockdowns like bandits crossing state lines. Every border felt like a win.

Eventually, we landed in Hilton Head.

Sun on our faces, air that didn't taste like fear. And that's where things shifted.

My husband encouraged me to get a set of golf clubs. I'd never played seriously a day in my life. But I figured, hey—why not? I bought a book. Taught myself to swing. Started whacking golf balls and falling in love with the quiet of it all. We stayed in a colleague's house, paid someone to drive the beast-of-an-RV back home, and just like that, what started as a nationwide shutdown turned into one of the wildest, most spontaneous, magical adventures of our lives. We were outside. Free. We were together. Socially distanced from the world—but so much closer to each other.

No plan. No expectations. Just fire pits, road maps, and the kind of memories you don't realize are magic until years later.

That's the art of timing. Time, interrupting the script because the script needs breaking, and time reminds you: You're not in charge. Yet something beautiful still is.

Timing is an art, not a science. Like all art, it's messy, mysterious, and full of surprises that don't make sense until you step back far enough to see the whole picture.

If I had never said yes to London—if I had trusted my better judgment instead of rolling the dice—my life would look completely different. I probably wouldn't have had more kids.

I wouldn't have opened the door to the wild adventure that came after that day. We did it anyway. We sold the house. We leapt, and as fate would have it, the house only got one showing. The kicker? It was a Monday morning. I wasn't ready. There was a poop in the toilet, a whole box of Tide had been dumped down the staircase. It was a disaster. The realtor tricked me into the showing, anyway, and that was the day we got well over our asking price. The people who showed up didn't want a showroom. They wanted real. They wanted to see the magic in the mess.

Picture this: Our three eldest kids were playing some wild game on the top floor of our townhouse in Beacon Hill. Next thing you know—

bam—our son's teeth go straight into our daughter's forehead. Screaming, crying, blood everywhere. They come downstairs looking like they've been in a cage fight. While I'm trying to stop the bleeding and assess if someone needs stitches, our third child—who was three at the time—is tearing through the kitchen like a tiny drunk monster. He slips, crashes to the floor, and yep . . . breaks his elbow.

So now, you've got one kid with a head wound, one with a broken arm, and one covered in tears and guilt because his face started it. That's the circus you bring to the ER when you're actually doing a decent job as a parent.

And let's be honest—anyone who hasn't been there? They're either not telling the truth, or they're due for it. Ladies and gents, the ones grinding it out, thinking they don't have grit:

Maybe you're a worrywart like I was. Maybe you want the perfect roadmap, the clean plan with every step mapped out. I remember the only book I ever picked up on parenting was *What to Expect When You're Expecting*.

And somehow, through the mayhem, I got some pretty damn amazing kids, too, kids with love and resilience, kids with grit, kids with independence, talent, spirit, and giant-hearted smiles. Don't get me wrong—I've made a full-blown roller coaster of mistakes.

Here's the thing: The foundation was built from love, and if that foundation is strong? Even the wildest, most weathered flower will bloom again. You bring the sunshine.

You bring the water, you plant the seeds, the rest? It'll take care of itself. You see, the ripple effect from that twenty-third mile still echoes, spreads, and influences.

It always brings me back to the start line—again and again—no matter how many times I've run it, no matter how much older I get, no matter how much life has thrown my way.

21

DIGGING IN TO DIG OUT

Safe keeps you upright. Sorry brings you to your knees. Sorry brought me to my knees, but do you want to know the truth? Every time I've found something real—love, purpose, the kind of joy that makes you cry—it comes on the heels of playing it sorry, of leaping when I wasn't ready or loving without a parachute or saying yes when my whole body was screaming no because it was scared.

That is the thing they don't tell you: safe will keep you dry, but sorry will baptize you. So you will have a choice all the time in life to pick. Safe or sorry. Comfort or story. Dry feet or a muddy, beautiful mess of a life. Me? I'll play it sorry, every damn time.

Our town burned down. I moved eight times in a row, with no idea what would happen in the next few years. My brother died suddenly, and I fully stopped running, training, sitting in my bathrobe for three weeks, crying.

My brother had been sicker than I really knew. I told myself he was fine because that's what you do when life feels like too much to carry— you let some threads go loose and hope they don't snap. During the fires, when the sky turned orange and the air stung like regret, he called me. More than once. I didn't call back. There was always something—

the kids, the smoke, the stress, the noise of trying to hold life together. And then he was in the hospital. A tangle of problems that got too big, too fast. His body gave out before I could get there. I said goodbye to him on FaceTime. A screen. He knew it was goodbye and groaned into the screen. Too much distance standing in for the human touch. He is the reason I'm writing this book. Every mile, every blister, every truth scraped out of me on the run is for him. Because some good has to come from the heartbreak you don't see coming.

I just stood on that 2025 Boston start line with his face taped to my bib, his children on my mind, and sick on top of it, with that ache in my chest that never fully goes away. Because that start line? It's a reminder: You never give up. My brother had a great, wicked sense of humor—sharp, quick, unforgettable. One of his favorite lines was always: "We're not gonna be having any of that now." We had made high school mischief together; we had some memories. This year, as I ran up mile eighteen, Heartbreak Hill, legs on fire, lungs tight, spirit flickering—I heard him. I stopped for a second, questioning whether I could keep going. I heard his voice, clear as day: "You get back out there and finish what you started, girl. We're not gonna be having any of that now."

When I first moved to California, right at the height of transition and emotional whiplash, I lost my mom to Alzheimer's. Her voice had already started slipping away from us before she passed. Aphasia took the words before the disease took her. But there were two sentences—two final messages—she managed to get out.

The first was when we had to move her to a memory care center. I begged her to try and like it. I needed her to settle in, to find some kind of peace. And she looked at me, clear-eyed, and said: "Because home is my place of being."

God. That one hit. And the second?

It was in Florida with her on the beach, her last trip with Dad. I was having a hard day, unraveling, tired of holding it all together. She looked right at me, the fog lifting for a second, and with full presence, said: "Stiff upper lip."

That was the last sentence my mother ever said to me. I love that woman. I carry her words with me everywhere. "Stiff upper lip" and

"Go outside to enjoy God's fresh air" certainly stuck. So yeah. Dig in because deeper isn't always darker. Sometimes, it's where the light finally gets in. Sometimes, it is forgiving yourself.

Digging in can give you perspective.

22

MY RIGHT-HAND MAN: THE ART OF LOVING LONG

I always dreamed of a relationship within a marriage that felt eternally emotionally connected. Through the good, the bad, the boring. I never wanted to get bored. I wanted a soul match. I got what I wanted. Not because I planned it, not because I knew exactly what I was doing. But because somehow, the universe handed me a partner who fit—not like a puzzle piece but like a cowriter in the margins of my life. After thirty years, it's still an awesome match. . . just in different ways now. Like the night of the fires. I didn't have to say a word, but he just knew—Kate's not going to be able to pack a suitcase right now, her brain is on fire too. So he turned the car around, racing the clock, thinking maybe he'd make it home just in time to do it for me. That's the kind of language we've built. No words necessary, just instinct.

And in this *long love* story—through all the moves throughout our thirty years—it only takes one sentence from him to shift the weight: "Yeah, Kate, I gotta head to New York for work. You know we've only got a week left in the month."

Translation: I know you're going to figure it out because you always do.

He's not perfect; he ducks and dodges and disappears on occasion. He's a little afraid of me when I'm in that mood—but he's also a master.

A magical master at doing the dance around timing, tone, and tact. He's learned—sometimes the hard way—when not to say things. Like, no more surprise trips. He tried. Oh, he tried, but eventually he realized he might end up at that romantic weekend solo. Still, he keeps trying, and so do I.

We keep learning from each other.

We keep dancing—even if the steps change every few years.

That's what makes thirty years still feel fun. Still feel alive.

Still feel like home. I'm talking about skating on the edge—real ice, real stakes. I'm talking about dancing down black diamonds at twenty-one, no money in the bank, no health insurance, and still blowing out your knee because you threw your body between me and the edge of a cliff, not metaphorically. Literally.

That's juice.

Love like that isn't just romance. It's the kind of love that packs your bag for you, books the hotel, and gently sends you off when your circuits are fried, and your soul is short-circuiting. No questions. Just, "Go. I got this."

It's making sure you get your miles in, even when life is stacked against you. That's ninety percent of the reason I was even able to write this book. Because I ran a lot of those miles alone, and only a man like him could understand that after enough quiet miles, enough held-in thoughts, eventually, something's gonna need to come out.

And when it did—when I turned to him a few weeks ago, wild-eyed and completely unfiltered, and said, "I think this is the time, I need to write a book"—he didn't flinch.

I could hear my brother's voice in the middle of the night, clear as day, like he was standing right there beside me. "Go start writing a book, Kate. You're a good writer." I heard him say it, serious and simple, the way only he could. And I knew he meant it. The truth is, in marriage—and in life—you spend a lot of time taking one for the team. You push your dreams to the side because someone's traveling, the kids need you, the house is loud, the bills are due, the laundry pile is high. There's always something.

I have been waiting to make the time to focus on just writing. Paul knew, you got to go do your thing now.

He just nodded because he knew. He'd seen it coming long before I had.

That's the kind of juice I'm talking about. Not the sweet kind. The strong kind. The real kind. The kind that keeps the fire lit and your story moving forward, even when you think you're running on empty.

I'm always fascinated by those couples—the ones who move through life like they've got their own silent choreography. You know the type. They smile with their eyes, finish each other's sentences, and make each other coffee without asking. They've done the work. The weaving. The repairing. The forgiveness. They've softened into each other over years, and maybe even decades. Me? So yes, it's been really messy. No, this chapter hasn't unfolded like a fairy tale. The fire stole everything we owned. Equity, photos, baby blankets, books, my favorite coat—gone. And while my insurance company, State Farm, ghosted me, I was sitting in a folding chair thinking, "Well, screw it. I might as well write a book."

Because even in the middle of the suck, there's still magic.

There was Big Sur under a blanket of stars in an RV I didn't know how to drive.

There was the Revel Race in Big Bear where the road froze. I nearly lost a toenail but found my spirit. I was watching my girls spike volleyballs and laugh with friends like they'd lived here their whole lives. There was my son graduating from Loyola with a cigar in his mouth and an aloha lei around his neck, flanked by his surfer crew who now call him. And now, there's a reformed garage in Manhattan Beach with a beat-up couch and string lights and a view of the sea that makes me forget what I've lost—if only for a moment.

See, relationships, love, and marriage aren't about having the same rhythm all the time. They're about learning to dance through the chaos, even when your partner's doing a waltz and you're doing the worm.

I am usually emotional, and he is rational. I am a lightning bolt; he is a steady current. He adapts like water. I hold on like a vice, and yet—when it counts—he shows up. He drives the damn RV even if he clips every curb in the cul-de-sac.

It was the day he sat on the edge of the bed and told me that both of our boys were gone. That sentence doesn't land easy, and it sure as hell didn't come out of his mouth without breaking something in both of us, but he did it with love. With tenderness. With hands that still held me even though his own world had just split wide open.

23

PARENTING AND PEOPLE SHOWING UP: COMPASSION

I didn't show up to parenthood with a backpack full of tools. I didn't even show up with a damn screwdriver. No grit, no grace— just hope, fear, and the belief that somehow, I'd figure it out as I went along. I never expected it to be what it is now, that is for sure.

The biggest myth about becoming a parent is that you'll know what to do. The truth? You don't. You just react, stumble, try, fail, cry, laugh —and somewhere between stepping on a Lego barefoot and pulling a kid out of a tree with a broken arm, you become a person who can withstand anything.

When the storm rolls in—because it always does—and your windows blow out and the whole house rattles and floods, you realize it's not about preventing the storm. It's about showing your kids how to walk through it. With your hair a mess. In sweatpants. With grace anyway. Grace isn't polite and polished in my house.

Grace shows up when your kid's elbow is cracked, your dog just died, your husband is on a plane, and you're still packing lunches. Grace means keeping a soft heart when everything else is falling apart.

Let me tell you: I didn't have any of that when I started. But parenting is the longest, hardest endurance race I've ever run. You think you need perfection to be a parent? You don't. You just need stamina. Humor.

You need a really good playlist and the ability to feel like you, even when you're about to fall, sit, or cry. You still pick up the mess with one hand while spoonfeeding a toddler with the other. Don't get me started on what it takes to stay soft.

Do not harden completely when the world keeps giving you gut punches. We all have our way through; some people see therapists. Good, do that. Some talk to friends. Beautiful. Do that too. But for the ones like me, who didn't have that luxury or just didn't want it—we dig.

It's not about wrapping your kids in bubble wrap and protecting them from the world. It's about letting them watch you weather it and showing them how to bounce back. And when you do it with love, even in your worst moments—that's how they learn strength. Every scraped knee, every heartache, every "I hate you, Mom" that turns into an "I love you" twenty minutes later is shaping the future of your family's emotional infrastructure. You don't have to get it all right. Just show up. Show up raw and messy and real.

You think you know what you'd do in a crisis until the crisis comes. You think you'll be resourceful, calm, maybe even heroic. But when you lose everything, and I mean everything, it's not about heroism.

It's about survival.

Survival is showing up at Target in pajama pants and sunglasses with no clue where to even begin. Survival is not knowing where you're going to live in a week, month, or even year while raising a family.

Survival is making do, leaning on the good people who care, finding the good in a hard situation, letting go, and adapting.

Just when you are a bit dazed, confused, and disoriented, people show up. Just when we think we know, we don't. Not just people I knew. People I didn't. People I met in parking lots, at distribution centers, strangers from Nextdoor who dropped bags on our porch or just looked me in the eye and said, "Hey. I got you."

Having doubts about L.A. or any move is real, I won't lie. It's a city of masks, filters, dream-chasers, and reinvention. I thought it was all about surface-level conversations and curated living.

But when the fire stripped us of everything, L.A. bared its soul. People opened homes, closets, pantries, wallets. People who didn't know my name remembered my face. And in those raw, burned edges of life, I saw the best side of humanity flicker into focus.

One woman, a total stranger—who by all means could've stayed a stranger—became family. She stood with me when my brother died; she also helped me furnish our little converted garage bedroom. She was there when I didn't even know how to be there for myself. No expectation. No performance. Just presence.

Next time you see someone fumbling through the ashes of their life —whatever those ashes may be—don't scroll past. Don't judge. Don't ask them to hurry up and be okay. Just sit with them. Offer them your time, your heart, your calm.

It's easy to take your inner circle for granted when you're stretched thin, exhausted, or lost in your own hard stuff. But it's also easy to learn. To change. To grow. To pivot. To choose better.

Because the truth is, money can buy a lot—nice houses, fancy cars, pristine golf courses—but it can't buy kindness. It can't buy genuine connection or warmth. In those shiny places, people are often wrapped in fear—not of outsiders but fear of vulnerability. Fear that if you let someone in, they'll see the cracks. The mess. The real human underneath the polished exterior.

These walls don't just keep people out. They trap everyone inside, stuck in their own small bubbles. Life isn't about the perfect lawn or the velvet rope. It's about messy kitchens and real conversations. It's about the kind of people who show up with open arms, not closed gates. The kind of people who include. The kind of people who know that community is about heart, not stature. And honestly, the richest people I know aren't the ones with the biggest bank accounts—they're the ones who make space for others, who share their table, who lift people up without a second thought.

So if you're in a place that feels cold and exclusionary, remember— it's not about you. It's about their fear and the loss they feel. It's not about you because real wealth is found in generosity, not exclusivity.

That's when your compassion gets legs. That's when your love starts running marathons. So pick up the phone. Knock on the door. Send the meal. Watch the kids. Write the real note. Don't just be "there" in name. Be there. You never know who's quietly unraveling behind the scenes. And you just might be the thread that holds them together.

Let's talk about the performance of compassion versus the real thing.

What is the real thing? It's showing up when it's ugly and inconvenient. It's sitting with someone in their shit storm without offering a hashtag. It's noticing.

It's the phone call instead of the "like." It's the walk you offer, not the walk you film.

And yet, so many people walk through this world with an armor of "I'm fine," because God forbid, they admit something's broken. The moment they do, they get branded—not with empathy but with a kind of polite distance. Like heartbreak or anxiety or divorce or loss or burnout is contagious. Like it's a moral failure.

But here's the truth: nobody's ever really fine. Not all the time. Not even most of the time.

Let's be honest: Many times we're all just covering bruises with good lighting. There's a whole subclass of people, club members who only RSVP to your life when it's good. When your kids are winning and your hair looks amazing, yet if you don't sing their songs, your teen gets suspended, your husband leaves, or you just stop smiling the way you used to?

You don't get dinners on your doorstep, do you?

You don't get invitations; you get silenced, ghosted. You get the Scarlet Letter version of motherhood, womanhood, personhood.

We need to stop confusing aesthetics with character.

Just because someone's living a pretty life online doesn't mean they're living a good one, and just because someone's struggling doesn't mean they're failing. In fact, those who struggle and still love, still give, still show up? Those are the ones I want and have in my circle. Those are the walkers. The ones who will lace up their shoes and meet you on the sidewalk when your world is collapsing, no cameras, no filtered selfies, just presence.

So if you're still reading this, and I hope you are, and maybe you've felt forgotten, ghosted, judged, or left behind because your story got sort of messy, know this: *You are not the problem.*

The problem is a culture that forgot how to care in a genuine way for even the little things. Forgot how to walk in another's shoes and hold grief. Forgot how to say, "Let me sit with you for a while."

Not the kind of friends I have. But there are many other circles and people we all see it in.

There are people who walk this world and shouldn't, not because they're evil but because they refuse to look anyone in the eye and say, "I see you. I've been there. You are not alone."

So let's be the ones who should walk this world. The ones who carry grace in our pockets and compassion on our tongues. The ones who make a little space at the table for the quiet, the hurting, the nonideal, and real peeps.

Because this life is not a highlight reel on Instagram, and we are not robots.

I'll really never understand the true mean-girl thing. The whisper campaigns. The side-eye circles of women who'd rather bash than build. You know the type—the ones who spend their energy knocking someone else down, when they could be offering a hand up. Women who hide behind curated lives, perfectly filtered moments, and cold indifference.

Not my gig. Why waste your time being nasty when you could be human?

If you've got a human heart beating in your chest, and you do, then you've got what it takes to understand someone else's pain, someone's story, someone's bad day. It takes something more than privilege or pedigree. It takes desire. You have to want to see things from someone else's point of view.

You have to want to lean in. It's easy to hide behind a fake wall of perfection. It's far harder but braver to show up real. I've seen what happens when women lift each other instead of judging each other.

I've lived it. The quiet coffee on a hard day. The text that says, "I've got you." The stranger-turned-sister who helps you rebuild or reframe a bad day or even your life from scratch.

Those are the kind of women I have gotten to know. Not the agenda or phony ones. The present ones.

When you're tempted to turn away from someone else's mess, try turning toward it. Not with judgment but with curiosity. With compassion. With a soft heart and an open mind.

Because real women don't tear down. *They lean in, lift up, and show the hell up.*

Because that's what we're born to do.

When you push yourself to the brink—when you challenge every cell in your body and every thread in your spirit—something cracks open.

For a good five years after my twins were born, I could only connect with a small circle of people. The ones who got it. The ones who didn't flinch when I told them the truth—that sometimes joy feels heavy, that sometimes healing is messy, and that it actually takes guts to smile when the world expects you to be bitter. There was one year that felt like the happiest of my life. And it made zero sense on paper. My daughter didn't get into a single school she applied to. Why? Because she had seventeen tardies before Thanksgiving.

Seventeen tardies. Why? Because I slowed our mornings down. We made breakfast. We laughed. We lingered. We chose joy. We packed two babies into the car and took our time. She was maybe twenty seconds late, maybe a minute—but we showed up smiling.

So yeah, life after the dream isn't always glamorous. Sometimes, you get the dream and still feel bruised.

Your journey? It's yours, but it can be magic in the mess.

Snowballs don't stop rolling just because you're happy.

Systems don't slow down to match your family's rhythm. People—institutions—still expect punctuality, order, rule-following. They don't care how many babies you're lugging in a car seat or how hard you fought to be present in that morning joy. And they certainly don't send thank-you notes for choosing presence over perfection.

That year . . . that year was a wild ride. It was the year my oldest son got a pacemaker. The same year the market crashed. It was the year I was nursing twins while helping two others with their homework and chasing another one down the street on a scooter. It was chaos, and it was beautiful.

The same year my mom and dad would come to visit two, sometimes three times a week. Somehow, in the middle of all that madness, I could feel how my presence, my messy, exhausted, centered presence—gave them peace. It helped them breathe a little easier. And that meant everything. Without saying it, they felt my joy, knowing all I had endured.

That was the year my angel friend Miranda from London—God bless her—just showed up one day in my apartment. No heads-up, no big announcement.

She just appeared, like the universe dropped her off at my doorstep. And sometimes that's how healing happens. In little, unplanned, grace-soaked moments.

In the friend who walks in the door at the exact second you forgot you needed someone. Healing doesn't look like spa days and bubble baths. Healing looks like that moment you choose to keep showing up anyway—when you choose joy despite the chaos, not because the chaos is gone.

It looks like Sunday dinners at my sister's house—the kind of dinners that feed more than just hunger.

She'd whip up magic in the kitchen while her beautiful dogs curled around the kids like living teddy bears. My crew would inhale her food like it was their last meal on Earth, and I'd breathe for the first time all week just walking through her front door. That's what love looks like in action.

She dropped off meals when I had busy weeks. She scooped up kids and filled in the blanks. There was the Patriots' Day parade, the laughter, the parties, the community—Boston in all its warm, gritty glory. It was a bubble of safety, of kindness, of infrastructure. A word that doesn't sound emotional until you realize it's the thing holding you up.

That's the world I left behind. Boston wasn't just about geography. It was a spiritual rip-out-by-the-roots moment.

I left my people, the ones who had my back, without needing to be asked. That warm, caring, messy, real-life village that you don't even realize is holding you together until you're standing in a place where no one knows your name. I won't lie. So far?

This next chapter hasn't exactly been a fairytale. Wildfires, losses, insurance battles, new terrain without the same net. It's been bumpy, it's been lonely, it's been a lot.

But I'm trusting it, holding out hope, and finding the good in every hour of the day.

24

MEMORIES ARE YOUR HOME

When I was a kid, I remember finding a bunch of pennies stuck to chewed-up gum in one of our drawers. Nobody else wanted to touch them. They were gross, stuck together, tossed aside like they didn't matter, but for some reason, I decided to pry them apart, clean them up, shine them up like little copper trophies. Then I made a piggy bank for them—an old coffee can or maybe a mason jar. I can't remember exactly. What I do remember is how good it felt to take something forgotten and useless and give it a little purpose. That day stuck with me. I felt bad for Mom some days; she had far more important things going on than to worry about thinking it planted the seed. And ever since, I've been drawn to the things other people overlook. The broken stuff, the worn stuff, the things that still have life left in them if you just pay attention. I repurpose, reuse, recycle—damn near everything I own, not just to save money, though that's a bonus. It's more about honoring the stuff we bring into our lives. It feels wasteful and weirdly disrespectful to treat things like they don't matter.

I've got clothes older than my own kids. Not in a trendy, vintage way—more like, "Hey, this shirt still fits, still works—why toss it?" It's a kind of rebellion, I guess, against mindless consumption. Against the idea that something loses value just because it's no longer shiny or new. Not just how to stretch a meal out of what's left in the fridge but how to see possibilities where others see nothing.

Love the little, neglected things because to me, it's hope, life, and creation.

That's where my magic is. The turkey bones making a soup, the ripped-up grocery bags, for tags, the stem of a flower replanted. It is when things that appear to have little life get extended.

So don't forget them. Don't downplay them if you've got some cool ideas and guts. Write them down.

This book brings me home because I am making stories of moments not to be forgotten and giving them a purpose. It's the way your dad laughed at your teenage antics, the way your kid looked at you like you held the moon. The way you survived the day you thought you wouldn't. No one gets to take those away.

That's why they belong in you. You are your home.

Because someday, when the wind blows a little too hard or the floor shakes under your feet, you'll need to remember: You've already lived a thousand miracles.

Joy isn't always clean. It doesn't wait for the perfect moment or a good hair day or a zero balance on your credit card. Joy shows up barefoot in the kitchen while you're dancing with your husband in pajamas that haven't seen the laundry in a week, morning breath and all. Joy is singing off-key when the house is falling apart, letting it go when the checking account is holding on by a thread, and when the days feel like a broken record spinning on high speed. You sing anyway. You move anyway. You fly anyway.

Transformation is not always some grand, cinematic epiphany. Joy, my style, is rebellion. Joy is grit with glitter. Joy is choosing to dance when life feels like a damn hamster wheel and realizing halfway through that maybe—just maybe—you've grown wings.

There's a funny thing that happens when the dust settles, the finish-line tape drops behind you, and your legs stop shaking from whatever marathon life just threw at you.

You start remembering.

Not just the hard parts—the heartbreak, the stretch marks on your soul, the burnt casseroles, or the squashed dreams you thought would grow wings. No, you start remembering it all. The snowballs of joy that snuck in on regular mornings. The chaos of a school drop-off that somehow felt sacred.

The one friend who showed up without asking.

The way your kid looked in a yellow slicker on a foggy London street corner. You remember. And that remembering? That's home. That is my home at least.

I left my real home—the warm, Irish Catholic, dog-filled, potluck, and Patriots' Parade kind of home—and ended up in a city of palm trees, wildfires, earthquakes, and strangers. I left my people, my church, my sister's football Sundays, all the things that held me together like stitches on a well-loved quilt. I traded it for what my husband's goals were.

For his new chapters and a somewhat shaky "what if." So maybe it didn't all work out, not yet anyway, but here's what I know now: You don't have to stay rooted in one zip code to feel grounded. You just need to stay rooted in your story.

We are living life, loving each other, and having fun anyway.

Nobody can take your memories. You carry them like medals around your neck. You carry them like songs stuck in your head. You carry them in the way you say "goodnight," in the way you watch your daughter braid her sister's hair, and in the shape of your own resilience.

25

GOLF, SHALL WE?

Califonia public golf is as public as golf gets.

No dress code, no fancy clubs. No stiff collars or khaki rules. You can show up in jeans and a T-shirt and nobody cares. You never knew who you'd get paired with—a retired mechanic, a tourist in rental shoes, some kid swinging like *Happy Gilmore*.

I was trying to find community. Trying to root myself into something normal, something familiar, something that smelled like home. I bounced—Rancho Park, Penmar, even a competitive ladies' team that promised connection and camaraderie but turned out to be more driving, more time, more effort than I had to give. If I was going to swing a club at all, it had to be simple. Easy. A public nine-hole.

No frills. No expectations. No damn performance pressure.

Just the feel of the grip in my hand, the quiet crack of the ball, and maybe—if I was lucky—a little peace.

When I couldn't get my shit together after we first moved to California, my husband would practically kick me or shove me out the door while he was working and needed peace to make me go play golf. "Go. Get some air. Swing a club. Do something that isn't thinking," he'd say.

One day, right after my mother got sick, I dragged myself to the course. I felt a little fuzzy. Like every cell was covered in fog. And there I was—stuck in the damn sand trap again.

I couldn't chip it out to save my life. A month before? Clean swings. Good rhythm. No problem getting the ball out. But that day? Nope. I chunked. I whiffed. I swore under my breath. "Damn it, why can't I hit the ball anymore? I just did this. What the hell is wrong with me?"

Next to me was this eighty-five-year-old man—thin, wiry, smooth swing—hitting the ball straight and long, longer than me, like it was the easiest thing in the world.

He must've heard me grumbling because he gently glanced over, smiled that slow, knowing smile, and said: "Don't you get it? We show up differently every day."

I found myself doing something I thought I'd really left behind in my twenties, then thirties, forties, now fifties: starting over. Here's the thing I've come to learn every time I get organized and try to make some master plan to feel fully in control. Life just laughs at me, interrupts me, and says, "When are you gonna wake up and stop trying to control things you can't?"

It took us an entire year to find our home. Two furnished rentals. Seven offers on homes to just buy a Taco Bell. Our Spanish villa on a hill sat empty for twelve years, tucked all alone above the Pacific Ocean on a platform of concrete. Inside was redone but without a soul, so we poured sweat and soul into it—the garden, the rooms, the spirit of the space.

And still . . . the transition wasn't easy. The real deal of starting over: Don't compare. L.A. isn't Boston. It's not cozy nor predictable, nor orderly, and it doesn't feel as safe. I still get lost easily every day, people beep, they look super beautiful, and are in a big hurry to upscale their lives. It's wide, spread out, a puzzle of neighborhoods with no history tying me into it.

You have to make the little things in life happen—the things that are only yours. Who knows your story? Only you, and it is one step at a time. Somewhere, you started hearing your own voice again. The one that says, *you belong too.* And that's the turning point.

Not when everything's perfect—it is interrupted most days—but when you realize you don't have to go back to what was to feel whole.

You just have to be willing. Willing to walk into the light with your heart cracked open, carrying the sun in your pocket, even if the ground still feels shaky. Because when you can feel joy and sorrow in the same breath—when you can make a home inside the ache and still choose wonder—you've tapped into something eternal. Home isn't where you started. It's where you decide to bloom next. That is your start line.

When your tank is empty, when the to-do lists stretch from here to eternity, when you're pouring into your husband, your daughters, your son, the house, the logistics, the damn lunchboxes, and you haven't heard your own name in your own head in weeks—that's when it gets real.

You don't wait for someone to knock; you get your hands dirty. You go out and buy a shitload of flowers. You dig a garden with tired hands and a heavy heart and build beauty with no audience.

You make something out of nothing. And that something—that tiny patch of joy, that bloom of color, that little moment where you created instead of collapsed—that's the starting line, the first breath of your comeback.

Because when you can give beauty even when you're getting nothing in return?

You've just proven to yourself that you're still here. Still in the fight. Still creating.

And that's how you start to draw people in—the real ones, not the performative types. The ones who show up with muddy shoes and hands full of seeds. The ones who water your soul while you water your garden, the ones who put out the fire in front of your house.

So maybe you don't "find" new friends in the usual ways. Maybe you build the kind of life that attracts the right ones. One petal, one shovel, one breath at a time. That's not just survival—it's art, and it is faith. That's grit and grace in bloom.

Who would've thought that same man on the wooden cross—the one you cried to, yelled at, maybe even ignored for a while—would show up again, not in some thunderous epiphany but in the quiet comfort of routine?

It's easy to lose faith when you've been burned, when your life's been packed in boxes or scattered by ash.

It's hard to trust again—people, places, systems. But sometimes, if you stay open long enough, if you let yourself be still and curious, something sacred slips back in through the cracks. And it might be through your children. Through watching them rise, shine, settle into new soil, and become leaders while you're still learning how to begin again.

So let the routine soothe you. Let the symbols and rituals anchor you. Let your kids' growth show you the path forward. Because maybe the wooden cross doesn't mean suffering—that raw, honest tumble through disorientation and motion.

The medicine is in the movement, and somehow, through all the wrong turns and dead batteries and cracked sidewalks, you found your footing.

Not because someone guided you there. But because you kept going.

That's the long run of transformation. Endurance.

You come from a place where roots run deep. Where your dad knows every crack in the sidewalk and honks at every neighbor because he belongs.

No storybook welcome mat. No parade. Just Sunset Boulevard throwing elbows—encampments, broken glass, lost souls with no one waving hello. And you're standing there with your history, your memory, your motherhood, your everything—getting muffled into bushes and wondering what the hell is happening.

That's culture shock with a side of heartbreak. Then—you meet her. That angel-friend who's lived here longer. Who doesn't hand you a fix but offers a frame. "It's just temporary," she says. "L.A. is in its *Lion King* era—the shadow part. The dark lands." And that hits differently. It lands because now you're not crazy or naive or missing something obvious; you're just walking through the hard part of the story. Every city has one—and every life too.

Here's the beauty: I kept walking anyway. Kept showing up with my wide-open heart and East Coast history, and little by little, the light came back in.

When the map you know stops working, walk anyway. Someone will eventually come along and help you rewrite it. Because that's exactly what you did. L.A. is teaching you how to know yourself by getting lost.

It's not just about getting lost—hell, getting lost is the easy part. It's about staying lost long enough to let the magic find you. And it always does. One construction worker at a time. One stranger, one sentence, one sideways moment that lands straight in your soul. "Change the way you look at things, and the things you look at change."

You asked for a sign, and the universe didn't give you fireworks or a billboard—it gave you a guy in a dusty vest outside the Getty Villa. A guy who looked you in the eye and unknowingly handed you a lifeline. That's what starting over really looks like.

It's not neat or pretty. It's you—aching for your kids who are far away, biting your tongue when your husband snaps, feeling invisible in a house full of eye rolls and silence. And still . . . you get up. You stay in it. You don't walk out. And every time you think you're breaking, someone —something—shows up to patch the crack. A neighbor. A friend. A sentence overheard. A little sign from the universe that says: "Don't quit on this. You're doing the hard part. And that's where the good stuff grows."

Because the truth is, when you're planting yourself in new soil, it always feels like nothing's happening. One day—you look up—and you're not just surviving. You're home.

After recently watching the Pacific Palisades' communities sprinkled around West L.A., Orange County, the Bay Area, kids in different schools, friends flying away like fairy dust—disjointed, grieving their prior lives—I can't help but feel an aching tenderness for them. These once-glimmering enclaves, with their manicured perfection and ocean-kissed air, seem to hold a collective memory of what used to be: neighborhoods where children played in the streets, hiking trails where neighbors knew each other's names, where time moved just a little slower. Now, they feel fractured. The smiles are polished but hollow.

Many families are feeling that their fuse is extremely short. Insurance is not coming through. Teen girl L.A. scene—the obsession with hair, nails, social schedules, the whole vanity vortex—is alive and well to keep distracted from the reality of displacement. I didn't really want this for my daughters. I wanted grit. Grounded. Boston grit, Charlestown edge, kids who grind. I wanted Latin School hallway stress and public transit lessons. Not at fifteen, the wardrobe wants. How am I handling it? I'm showing up to the page to create a new memory instead of checking out. I'm writing. I'm doing something about it. I know because when you feel stuck, movement is everything.

Just one step. One sentence. One deep breath. Action, moving, changing it. Parenting through culture shock—where identity, stability, and love are all thrown into flux.

We had only lived in our home for two years. The night of the fires, the fire map told us everything was gone. The wind flipped backward toward the water, then suddenly shifted. That red swirl of flame had a pulse of its own. It didn't follow the rules. It didn't matter that we had just planted a garden after two years of patience. That we had built a volleyball court out of sweat and teenage joy. That the front bushes were finally growing into the hedge I'd always imagined. But fires don't ask questions; they take. And yet somehow—somehow—our house stood. And when that Green Beret called me, ready to charge back into the smoke and grab what mattered most, I didn't think of my jewelry box or photo albums. That place, that fire, it taught me this: You can lose the building. But if you remember the people—you keep the home. The fire burned the bushes and the hill and the sacred steps that led us to community. But it couldn't burn what we had already built inside. It couldn't take the mornings in the choir, the way they remembered me by name, the way we remembered each other's stories.

That's what makes a place yours. Not the kitchen cabinets. Not the paint color. But the way someone looks at you and says, "I'm glad you're here." It wasn't the fact that our house didn't burn.

After the fire, we had people who showed up to stand in the ashes with us; somehow, that's when L.A. started to feel like home.

But that's where imagination comes in. That's where a little sweat and heart and community can stitch you back together again.

That's when you get to build something new.

Corpus Christi—the place that held my grief, baptized my joy, celebrated my daughters—had to scatter. But like dandelion seeds on the wind, it found new soil. They became a traveling parish, visiting all the sweet, simple churches tucked into this big, messy city. Each Mass was like spiritual cross-training. A reminder that holiness isn't rooted in one address. It's wherever love is present.

Here's the funny thing about thinking you've got it all figured out: life has a way of shaking that snow globe just when you've settled the flakes. I used to pride myself on being in the know—on reading the room, managing the chaos, holding it all together with a smile and a plan. But when you hang your identity on certainty, life will find a way to humble you.

My dad, though—he's always brought this steady calm into my life. Security. Simplicity. He speaks in a language that makes sense. That old-school, dry wit kind of sense. And I'll never forget this one day on the beach in Scituate. Every summer, we've sat at the same spot for as long as I can remember—same folding chairs, same iced coffee, same tide creeping in.

We're looking around, and he nods toward a family nearby, and he says, "Yeah, sad they're not talking to each other anymore."

And I laughed, like—how could that happen?

Families talk. That's what we do. Except, a little while later, it happened to us.

How do we make ourselves feel at home when we are not *in* our home?

The Palisades Fire became the most destructive wildfire in Los Angeles history, fueled by hurricane-force Santa Ana winds and prolonged drought conditions. You would have to see it to believe it. Looking at it now, the fire scorched over 23,000 acres, destroyed more than 6,800 structures, and claimed twelve lives.

Entire neighborhoods, including the Pacific Palisades, Topanga, and Malibu, are unrecognizable. I remember standing on my porch, watching the sky turn an eerie orange, the air thick with smoke, smelling burnt wood, and hearing the sound of sirens filling the atmosphere. It was a stark reminder of nature's power and the fragility of our human constructs.

The fire didn't just consume homes; it tested everyone's resilience. Many communities came together, offering shelter, food, and support to those affected. It was in these moments of crisis that I witnessed the true strength of human connection. This chapter isn't just about the physical fire but also the metaphorical fires we've all faced—loss, fear, and uncertainty. It's about how we rise from the ashes, rebuild, and find meaning amidst chaos.

I have learned that closed doors can be the opening to the breakthrough.

You, too, can endure the moments when nothing seems to be going your way; adapting and growing through setbacks is really key.

If you can see them as just part of the special design made for you, it will make a major difference. The narrow faith, patience, and purpose-driven action. Let's walk together to confidence, clarity.

The patterns and logic are obvious. Why is it not happening for me?

What if the closed door was a redirection? People who rise above the noise are the ones who rise above it. Setbacks are part of the grand design. Frustration is looking at what we don't have and walking through the forest with our eyes closed.

Dozens of doors are waiting for you to open them, yet many times we don't see them. I, personally, have had to tap into this since the fires.

Growth happens in the waiting room of life.

Your path is unique; nobody else has it.

Impatience is a trap. Make poor choices, and wind up in places you don't belong.

Two years after planting myself into this new life, the land went up in flames.

The California fires in the Pacific Palisades should've broken me or phased me, but they didn't. They are just another mile twenty-three.

Losing the material belongings isn't the same as losing meaning. Grief taught me to let go of expectations long before I ever moved here. The hardest part of coming to California wasn't the fire. It was losing my mother and brother. It was learning—again—that we don't get to script our lives, yet we do get to decide how we respond to them. Every time I've lost something . . . people have shown up. Find your people who show up for you—and do the same for them.

Home isn't a place.

It's just a presence. It's what we bring to it—the life, the spirit, the we.

Our home in the Pacific Palisades became a mirror of my soul: I learned to be a gardener—not just of plants but of memories. I poured my grief into the soil, dedicating trees and spaces to the ones who had gone before me. And somehow, these little dedications became relationships. Quiet bonds of joy, remembrance, and unexpected healing. The structure of a home is not what makes it sacred. But the people do. The energy does. The *we* inside the walls is what matters. And just as I began to feel rooted . . .

OK, now well . . . the town burned down.

I look forward to problems today. I expect them to build a different kind of resilience now. I used to freeze—maybe flake or crumble under decision fatigue, put pressure on myself to have it all "figured out." This life taught me something wild:

Life will pull everything else out from under you—your plans, your routine, your comfort zone. *But your attitude?* One day at a time. That's the thread you can still hold onto.

Parenting through a culture shock is like trying to build a home while the ground shifts beneath your feet. You're not just raising children—you're translating an entire world to them, even as you struggle to understand it yourself. The seven moves with new beds, spaces, the language, the subtle codes of behavior—they all feel foreign, not just to you but to the version of yourself you used to be.

There's beauty in that dissonance too. There's a certain strength in raising children while a little disoriented yourself. It is OK. It teaches humility. It strips away pride. You become more present. You listen more, and you learn with them—and often from them. The power dynamic shifts, and love stretches wider to accommodate new definitions of home, of safety, of identity.

You watch them create hybrids of culture—and you realize that culture shock is not just something to survive. It's something to parent through.

With grace, humor, and acceptance that the map you grew up with may no longer apply—but that doesn't mean you're lost.

It just means you're evolving. Yet I will admit—if I must look at Waze again and learn a new landmark saying "home," forget it.

Culture shock doesn't hit all at once. It's slow, cumulative—like water wearing down stone. You lose things quietly.

26

THE BRIGHT SIDE OF KIND
STRANGERS IN THE DARK

I signed the lease in the dark.

Not metaphorically. I mean it was night, and I couldn't see a thing. I had no idea where I really was. I just knew I needed a place to land.

Needed to feel like life wasn't fully unraveling, even if it was pulling at the seams.

I needed a zip code I could plug into delivery apps and a place I could cook without a new learning curve.

So, we said yes.

Manhattan Beach.

We needed a home now, and the air in the Palisades is unhealthy and toxic, filled with chemicals.

We could endure anything for a year.

But here's the thing nobody tells you about running toward survival: Sometimes, if you're lucky—or maybe just open enough—you don't land in survival. You land in joy.

Not all at once. Not in a parade. It sneaks in through the cracks. A neighbor who waves every time you pass, even when you're looking down at the people who say hello here.

A walk to the ocean, where you suddenly exhale in a way you forgot your body could. A beach that isn't for showing off—but for show-ing up.

I didn't know Manhattan Beach would be so special.

Didn't know it was a place where people smiled back. Where kids rode bikes like it was 1992. Where strangers looked you in the eye, not to size you up but to see you. This town doesn't walk past you with AirPods and attitude—it walks with you. Literally, it's a walking town. People meet in motion. Dogs in tow. Sand in shoes. Life happens in real time, not behind gates.

It's like the universe dropped me here—after the fires, after the chaos, after the bombs and the breakups and the breakdowns—and said: Try this. Try light. Try laughter again. Try community, connection, clarity—even if it's only for a year.

We came in the dark, and, somehow, we were met with light.

And yes, this town has its quirks. Parking is an Olympic sport. The air smells like sunscreen and ambition. And I've seen more golden retrievers in one block than I'd seen in my entire East Coast life.

But it works. It works in a way that feels undeserved and wholly sacred. Like someone left the door open to grace, and I happened to wander in.

I don't know what'll happen after the lease is up. I don't know if we'll stay or go.

But I know this: I came here burned out, broken open, unsure if anything would grow again. And here, somehow, joy did.

So maybe that's the gift in the fire. Not just the cleansing. Not just the survival. But the chance to find yourself in a place you didn't plan for, surrounded by people you didn't know you needed, and surprised by love you never saw coming.

After the fires took the town up in a blaze, it was survival mode on the go, without a plan of where, how, what to do—one hotel, another, a VRBO, a kind woman who gave us her home, back to another hotel. And then, due to me opening up and telling the real estate broker a little more about ourselves, she worked a bit harder and remembered us, despite the thousands of others looking to sign leases and get settled. So she realized I didn't need big nor fancy and preferred an empty space with light, which is what she showed me one fuzzy evening. I did not care. I said, "Yes."

The storm got stronger. When we finally found a long-term rental —an empty, dusty, half-finished space—I saw it at night. I expected to start from scratch, so my plan was to collect mattresses. Folding chairs. Cold echoing rooms, figuring I would go to Salvation Army and Facebook Marketplace. I'd find some decent low-cost furniture. As the month of February went by, I collected some inexpensive items in hopes of making it feel more like home. Yet when I opened the door, I found furniture, family photos, artwork, and comfy beds.

It was a home I would've designed myself. And it was all there because of the kindness of a total stranger. A total stranger who heard a story about a family she did not know and filled the space with warmth, soul, and grace, which took a lot of work, hustle, time, and planning. And although she had an extremely busy life of her own, she made us the priority.

That's why I wake up every day full of faith in humanity. Not because life has been easy—because people are good.

It is strange. I am kind to people for no reason; it sort of drives my kids crazy. I take time for random people, but everywhere I tend to go— planes, escalators, checkout lines, elevators—people just tell me things. I love it. I like giving to people, not because I'm nosy, but because I get to witness people in their most honest form. Because something in me says, "You're safe here. Speak freely."

For example, there was this girl I found once, stumbling barefoot through our neighborhood in the Palisades. A little lost, a little out of it —she ended up passed out on the side of the road not far from our house. But her nails? Perfect. Freshly done, glossy, like she'd just stepped out of a salon.

She needed help. And somehow, I became that help.

It didn't stop there. It never does. I became that person—on hikes, on airplanes, in grocery store lines, waiting for luggage—strangers pouring out their life stories like I'd hung a sign around my neck that said *Tell Me Everything.*

Hours and hours of other people's stories. Joy, heartbreak, drama, dreams. Like some accidental grief whisperer . . . or maybe just a tired mom who looked like she'd listen.

The list goes on. And on.

I hope my kids do what they can for others as they grow; there is a lot more joy in giving without wanting anything in return. Because when is it time to execute? The preparation is what carries you through.

We raise them to be strong, to be themselves. To chase things we only dreamed of. But nothing prepares you for the moment they actually go. That moment you realize they don't need you the same way anymore—but they still carry you in how they think, speak, live.

August 8, 2023

Nantucket Island:

I woke up, looked at the storm on the ocean, and said, "Mom's going to die real soon." Then my sister called and said it was time.

I quietly explained to my twin girls that Nana wasn't going to be with us much longer. That she was getting ready to go.

We didn't have a car on the other side of the ferry. I was already bracing for the next set of hurdles—how we'd get home, how I'd keep it together.

Then a woman—someone I didn't know, someone I'd never see again—turned to me and said: "I'm sorry, I overheard your conversation. My mother died twenty-five years ago today, and I'd like to drive you to your hometown. Please let me. Let me thank you."

I had no words. Just stunned, grateful silence. She didn't owe me anything. She had nothing to gain. She simply listened. She heard the love in our conversation. And something in her said: *Go to them.*

And she did.

There are people like that.

People who show up for you in a single moment and change everything.

Or my mother, slipping away from this world on the exact same day my sons did: August 9.

Life gives. Life takes. Sometimes, in the exact same breath. You can't plan it. But you can pay attention. They are never random.

They're the secret stitches in the fabric of our own beautiful life. Like the tattooed Roman numeral seven on my kids' ankles.

The threads you can't see but can always feel.

People who are sent.

Like the ones who send you a hand-painted box that says, "God will never take you to a place that His grace can't protect you in."

Or the girl who showed up with flowers on the top of a hike and flew far just to see you.

The construction worker who tells you to change how you look at things when you share on a whim you're having a tough day.

The two trees planted in my backyard? The women who stand by them are angels too.

For the ones who showed up with pennies and patience and presence.

Thank you.

That woman.

Those people.

My people.

Do you walk around with those types of people in your life? Are you even aware of them? Do you make room for them, notice them, water those roots? Or have you been so wrapped in the noise, in the grind, that you've mistaken flashy for faithful?

Because these people—they're the real wealth. The quiet ones. The faithful ones. The ones who just show up. And maybe the bigger question is: Are you one of them?

Here we are again—on another path I never expected. A new dirt trail.

Wood chips underfoot.

Somewhere between Manhattan Beach and Hermosa.

Blue-eyed grass sways next to California poppies—native, wild, unapologetically beautiful.

It's not my garden.

But it's here for me anyway.

A garden for me to enjoy, to breathe in, to learn from.

Life has taken me through so many spaces and places I didn't plan to go.

And still—there's beauty.

Even in the middle of a path I never chose.

Walk, breathe, appreciate, and remember to say . . .

You've got to smell the roses while they last.

And, if possible, be entertained in the process.

I hope this book gives you a practical lens to think about your kids, your partner, your aunt, your boss, your friends—whoever's part of your ecosystem.

How to navigate challenges in a way that isn't boring, performative, or overly academic.

Life is often a complete cluster of confusion, but it doesn't have to stay that way in your heart and head.

This book is for the real ones. The wandering ones. The ones who want to make sense of the mess, get through the hard stuff, and still feel grateful, beautiful, and content—even while it's still hard.

Your mile twenty-three results will also only come from focus.

So feed your mind, build your vision, and strengthen your why.

Decide this is the year. The best one yet. Make a commitment—not just to dreams but to doing.

I woke up a month ago and said: *This is it. I am done with loose ideas.* I said I wanted to write a book, thanks to a little nudge from a friend. I did not ask permission; I took it. I went to the library and locked myself away for thirty buzz days, twelve hours a day, to complete what I started half-heartedly—because people need other people to share what is real and how they truly coped with hard things.

Remember this:

You can watch the parade.

You can join the parade.

Or you can create your own and lead it.

Sam and Myles's tree

The finish line to qualify for London's World Marathon Majors, 2023.

First Christmas back in Boston as a family of five.

Our neighborhood in the Palisades—2024.

January 7, 2025, Evacuation Day

My brother Gerry.

www.ingramcontent.com/pod-product-compliance
Lightning Source LLC
Chambersburg PA
CBHW051619120626
46551CB00014B/1862